POPULAR

POPULAR

BOYS, BOOZE & JESUS

a memoir

TINDELL BALDWIN

TYNDALE HOUSE PUBLISHERS, INC.
CAROL STREAM, ILLINOIS

Visit Tyndale online at www.tyndale.com.

TYNDALE and Tyndale's quill logo are registered trademarks of Tyndale House Publishers, Inc.

Popular: Boys, Booze, and Jesus

Designed by Mark Anthony Lane II

Published in association with Yates & Yates (www.yates2.com).

All Scripture quotations, unless otherwise indicated, are taken from the Holy Bible, *New International Version*,® *NIV*.® Copyright © 1973, 1978, 1984, 2011 by Biblica, Inc.™ Used by permission of Zondervan. All rights reserved worldwide. www.zondervan.com.

Library of Congress Cataloging-in-Publication Data

Baldwin, Tindell.
   Popular : boys, booze, and Jesus / Tindell Baldwin.
      pages cm
   ISBN 978-1-4143-7524-3 (sc)
1. Baldwin, Tindell.   2. Christian biography—United States.   I. Title.
   BR1725.B3335A3 2013
   277.3'083092—dc23
   [B]   2012040419

Printed in the United States of America

19   18   17   16   15   14   13

7   6   5   4   3   2   1

Dedicated to my husband for looking at me as Christ sees me and not at my jaded past, and to my family for showing me what unconditional love looks like.

Contents

Introduction

Welcome to me.
I'm going to give all my secrets away.

HELLO, I HOPE you're listening. . . .

I'm sitting at the Austin airport stuffing my face with overpriced candy, all in the name of PMS, and wondering how I'll ever be able to write a book for teenage girls. The topics seem too vast and too graphic to really dive into, and yet I have an intense desire for teens to swallow some truth along with all the other messages being sent on a daily basis.

This dream began when I was twenty and spent the summer interning at a Christian youth camp. I'd only recently come out of my dark world of booze and boys, and I realized that my story was like so many others. When I shared my story with the teens at the camp, they opened up, they took it in, they understood. That's when it hit me—my story was relevant because it's the story of life after a battle. It's the story of what happens when God reaches down and saves us from the thick of it. I'd danced with true turmoil and lived to tell the tale. So that became my goal: just to tell a story—a story that resonates with teens where they are.

For so many, high school is a blur of bad decisions, followed by college, which is an even bigger blur of bad decisions (but these don't require your parents' permission), and then you're thrown out into the world. Eventually, we all wake up and realize we need a Savior. My thought behind this message is that you won't have to wait so long before you realize your deep need. My hope and my prayer is that truth will speak louder than the lies the world is feeding you.

The younger you are, the greater the distractions are. That's why it takes us so long to realize how much we need God. There are so many things that keep our minds away from Him: technology, social networking, TV, movies, books (but not this one, of course!). With so many enticing distractions, it can take years to learn that these things will not make you happy, and neither will the next thing, or the next.

What I never realized when I was younger, and what I hope to reveal now, is that the decisions you make when you're seventeen will shape the way you live the rest of your life. Who you sleep with will be in your heart forever. The addictions you form at fifteen won't go away on your twenty-fifth birthday, and cleaning up your life doesn't magically happen. I wish someone had told me this. My hope is that these pages are filled with things you've been wishing someone would tell you.

It was hard for me to see that I needed God. When I was sixteen and all my friends were drinking, it was easy to think, *Why shouldn't I?* Then I was seventeen and all my friends were having sex and seemed to really be in love, and it was easy to think, *Why shouldn't I?* There were plenty of reasons why I thought I didn't need God in high school and college: my life was filled with distractions that pushed Him to the side, and He was asking me to give up things that seemed very appealing. He was asking me to refuse the things that felt good, looked good, and tasted good.

God is still asking a lot from teenagers. He is asking them to be different, and asking most fifteen-year-old girls to be different is like asking them to grow beards.

The truth is, a lot of things are just distractions, designed to keep us happy for a little while, until the next "latest and greatest" thing comes out. I'm a huge iPhone advocate. I love my current iPhone, but I know as soon as Apple comes out with the next generation of the iPhone, I'll most likely "need" it. Life's distractions are things that keep us happy for a while so we don't realize how unhappy we really are. I'm not against technology, I'm not against progress, and I'm not against Apple. I'm against these things distracting us from our need for a relationship with our Creator, a need to be in creation, a need for human contact, and a need to be fulfilled by something greater than this earth can offer.

I love having an app for everything, and I'm not blaming society's problems on Facebook. I'm just saying distractions make things harder for us. It's harder to get away, harder to concentrate, and harder to get our attention. Why? Because *everything* wants our attention.

There's so much to do, so many things to play with, e-mails to check, videos to watch, music to listen to. When was the last time you sat in silence for more than a few minutes? It feels weird. We're constantly surrounded by video, music, people. No wonder attention-deficit/hyperactivity disorder is more prevalent than ever; no one has to concentrate for more than thirty minutes to learn everything they need to know. You almost need to have ADHD to keep up with society. When I drive, I'm always doing at least two things (sorry, Mom): eating on the go, checking my phone, talking to a friend, all the while looking at my GPS. The distractions are everywhere—how can God break through all the streaming media?

I've been trying to answer this question for a long time. After I became a Christian, I started to see the wreckage that came from my four years of partying, and I wanted to give girls something to help them navigate life. I wanted to convey that hope lies on the other end of the road. Walking through high school is like walking in the woods with a flashlight—you can only see so far ahead. I have been there, and I might be able to cast a little extra light on your trail. I might be able to stop you before you chain yourself to choices you will live with for the rest of your life.

I get the feeling people often give up reaching out to the younger generation and hope to catch them on the upswing. For me this felt very true. It didn't feel like a whole lot of people (besides family) wanted to love me where I was; they wanted me to change before they would consider reaching out to me. Well, part of the reason I'm writing this book—the main reason—is that I want to catch you on your downswing. I want to send you a message of hope in some of the darkest days of your life, because changing the direction of your life right now might be just what this world needs.

Usually, high school marks every big moment in your move from childhood to adulthood: first kiss, first car, first car wreck, first love, and the first time you have to decide who you are. In high school you step as far out from under your parents' roof as you can while still living there, and you attempt life on your own. It's a trial-and-error process that type A personalities pass with flying colors, but people like me . . . well, we crash and burn and thank God that His grace abounds.

I want to write this book with the kind of utter honesty that makes people uncomfortable. That might sound weird, but until we're brutally honest about important issues, we won't know how to tackle them. This means I'm going to put a lot of deeply personal stuff in these pages in hopes you can learn from some of my mistakes. If you're anything like me, the temptation will be to prove me wrong, to prove you can do what I did without ending up in a downward spiral. I hope you won't try. While you might be fortunate and come out with only a few deep gashes, you might not be. I've been to plenty of funerals for people who didn't have the luxury of second chances. I've watched friends go to rehab fighting to break the chains of addiction, and I've watched others not able to give it up at all. So I hope you won't try to prove me wrong. I hope through my story you'll see what I had to learn the hard way: we all need a Savior.

DARK

CHAPTER 1

WHERE IT ALL BEGAN

I'M 794 MILES from my hometown, but somehow it all feels so familiar: the lockers, the overwhelming smell of vanilla and Abercrombie, the confusing layout, the kids rushing to class, the couple in the corner making out. I walk the halls and breathe a sigh of remembrance. The bell brings me back to the here and now, and I have no idea where room 2070 is.

Finally I stumble into the classroom, and twenty sets of eyes look at me. A few of them look confused; I'm obviously not their teacher. I tell them that today I'm their substitute. A few more confused looks, and then one brave girl in the back asks, "How old are you?"

"Twenty-three," I say, looking down at my instructions. They have a test today.

"You look like you're eighteen," one of the pretty girls in the front says.

I glance up and see the familiar scene. It might be six years since I was in high school, but not much has changed. There's still the loner in the back wearing all black, trying to blend in with darkness; the oversize scary boy who wants me to know I don't have authority; the peppy cheerleader who smiles even when nothing is happening; the angry girl who probably dates the scary boy in row three; the athletes who swish their hair to the side trying desperately not to care; and the rest: the average-for-now kids who get lost between categories. I know they won't take their test until I go through the normal ritual of questions, so I let them ask.

No, I didn't go to school here, and yes, I'm old enough to teach. Yes, I'm super tall, and no, you may not stand next to me to see if you're taller. No, I didn't play basketball, and yes, I'm married. By this point I can normally get them on task, but the brave girl in the back says something I don't expect.

"Tell us your life story."

I look up. Twenty sets of eyes look back. Only forty-five minutes left in class. I wish I could tell them my life story.

I would tell the popular girls to be nice, because later in life they'll realize life isn't about them. I would tell the pretty girls that looks aren't all they have. I would tell the kids in black that this is just a phase and the real world isn't quite so harsh. I would tell the tough girls that getting hurt is part of life. I would tell the pretty boy with the hair swoosh that there will be a million of him wherever he goes next and the only thing that will make him stand out is his character. I would tell the girls trying desperately to fit in that one day it won't be so hard. I would tell the in-betweens that one day they'll have their place in this world. Mostly I would tell them there is a Jesus who loves them, a Jesus who knows what they are going through and has a relationship waiting for them that is more than they could ever imagine. There are so many things I would like to tell this class, but for now they have to take a test.

So which one was I? Great question. After I watched *Mean Girls* with my parents when I was sixteen, my dad turned to me and asked, "So, which one are you?" I was Lindsay Lohan's character: a little clueless, but drunk with the idea of being on top of the popularity food chain. I had started off as a no one, but because of a late burst of puberty and my ability to take shots of vodka, I was fumbling my way to the top, making all the classic mistakes along the way.

I was like many teenagers. I hated my parents. I drank alcohol. I smoked weed and the occasional cigarette, had sex, got a broken heart, struggled with depression, and in the end wanted out. I have a classic high school story but with one big twist at the climax. Here's where it began:

Before the alcohol, the hookups, the rebellion, and the aches and pains of teenagedom, I was just a little girl with two parents I adored and three brothers I wanted to be like. There was a time before puberty when I enjoyed being with my family. A time when I still laughed at my brothers' singing. A time when we would catch turtles at Hilton Head. A time before my dad became embarrassing and we still played games together on Friday nights. We were all best friends in the time before life took hold of me and I became *too cool*.

My dad would come to call the time when I became *too cool* the "blue eye shadow phase" because I wore a thick layer of blue eye shadow up to my eyebrows, and I thought it looked good. (If you're in this phase, do us all a favor and throw away the blue eye shadow. It doesn't look good.) It seemed the more eye shadow I wore, the witchier I got, and my parents bore the brunt of my hatred. I started drinking because I thought I deserved the freedom to drink. It was my parents' fault my life was so hard, and if they'd just let me do what every teenager does, then we wouldn't have any problems. If they'd just let me stay out all night and drink, even though I was underage, we would be okay.

When I was sixteen, I went through a phase where I refused to tell them I loved them. I thought I could prove how much I didn't need them if I only withheld my love. I would storm off to bed, angry about something I didn't have that I desperately needed, but they'd just smile and say, "I love you." The little girl inside me longed to say it back, knowing I needed them more than ever at this time in my life, but I refused her.

All this denial, anger, hatred, and need were compounded by the fact that my mom was sick. Her first "episode," as we came to call them, happened when I was four. She had a fever and chills and could barely get out of bed. We took her to the hospital, and I remember my dad buying us Happy Meals and letting us play in a park nearby. The doctors told her she was dehydrated and gave her some fluids. But it wasn't dehydration. The episodes came back again and again, and they continued for the rest of my childhood. The doctors would think they were close to an answer, and then it would slip away.

The only time my mom and I got along was when she was sick. That's when I became her caretaker. I brought her ice packs when her headaches were unbearable, ginger ale when she wanted something to soothe her stomach. I folded laundry when she was too weak to manage. This was the only time I made life easier for her. Sometimes, when she was really sick, we'd sit on her bed and watch TV, just enjoying moments of peace. In a way, her sickness brought healing moments to our relationship, but it was also hard. At ten, I knew the grocery store like the back of my hand. I could cook dinner and often did. When my mom was sick, no plans were definite, and I got used to shopping trips being canceled, activities being moved, and life being put on pause. It wasn't anyone's fault, but when you're a kid, you don't understand that, and I adjusted to her chronic illness like all kids adjust to change, kicking and screaming.

Being my mom's caretaker and getting used to having my needs put on hold is probably why I became fiercely independent. And it's at least partly why I cheated on all my boyfriends one way or another until I was eighteen. I had to prove I didn't need them, that I was stronger than they were. I had to prove to myself that I was beautiful and worth being wanted, and I had to prove to others that nothing fazed me. I didn't care who I left in the ashes as long as I came out okay. Of course, this was a shell—a way to hide how deeply insecure I was and how much I really wanted to be loved.

When I was fifteen, I got a necklace from my cousin that said "Rebel" on it—*very* classy. I wore it with pride, hoping it would confirm the rough exterior I put on. I wanted everyone to know that I needed no one. But that was the furthest thing from the truth. I needed love, I needed attention, I needed a place to belong, and most of all I needed to know who I was. So I created who I was—I made myself the person I'd always hoped I could be. I followed rules I created for myself, strict social guidelines that would ensure

I always came off as cool. As a sign of my true strength, I acted like nothing bothered me. In fact, I stuffed away all the pain that came with being a teenager. I stuffed away the pain of disappointing my parents and losing friends, the pain of rejection, and the pain of guilt. From the outside I appeared happy, healthy, and loving life, but on the inside I was praying no one would find out I was a fake.

The thing that drove every decision I made at this point of my life was my desire to be part of the popular crowd. I was scared and insecure in who I was, so I sought to belong to a group that seemed to know exactly who they were. There were no limits to what I would try. I would be whoever anyone asked me to be as long as I was a part of the crowd. I drank because that's what you did when you were popular. I smoked weed because to be cool you had to at least try it. I fooled around with boys because that's what the other girls did. I didn't know who *I* was; I just knew who I wanted to be like.

The first time I got in trouble for drinking, I was fifteen and went to party with some of my older brother's friends and my best girlfriend at the time. My parents were out of town, and I told my grandparents I was going to a friend's house. When I walked in, everyone stared in disbelief and delight, and they immediately started offering me drinks. Some of my brother's friends were fighting over who could give me shots. No one could believe that I, a member of the Stanfill family, wanted to get drunk, so they watched in anticipation as I drank shot after shot. Before I knew it, I was wasted and had made out with my best girlfriend at the older boys' urging. I don't remember it, but a picture truly says a thousand words. By the end of the night I'd also made out with one of my older brother's friends, even though I had a boyfriend—another picture memory—and was hanging my head over a toilet seat in the arms of a stranger. My boyfriend at the time found out and was livid. He tried to call me, but I wasn't answering my phone. Everyone was in a panic trying to figure out whether I needed to go to the hospital or not, but I wouldn't let them take me, because I knew I'd be in trouble. The night ended when I stumbled home and fell into bed with the stale taste of vomit on my breath.

On Monday the whole school was talking about what an idiot I'd made of myself. I was mortified. My boyfriend broke up with me, and when my parents came home they got four phone calls from "concerned parents" letting them know what had happened. My parents confronted me, and I'll never forget my dad asking me why I made out with my girlfriend. How could I explain to him that I would do anything for the popular kids, even if it meant making a fool of myself?

I was grounded for three months. Much of my freshman year continued in this manner: groundings, followed by freedom, followed by drunken nights, followed by loss of trust and another period of being grounded. It was an endless cycle I couldn't escape. My parents tried every bargaining tool in the book, but I wouldn't give up alcohol for anything. One spring break my mom even let me get my belly button pierced because I told her I'd quit drinking if she did. I lied. I didn't think I could be cool without alcohol, and I couldn't survive if I wasn't cool. My reasons for drinking were all lame, but somehow I kept convincing myself they were valid. Self-exploration was my favorite excuse, although I don't know how much you can find out about yourself with your head hanging over the toilet.

I'm an all-or-nothing person, which explains why I felt the need to try everything before my sixteenth birthday. I was in my best friend's basement when I first smoked marijuana. (First moral of the story: parents, don't get a house with a basement.) We were bored on a Friday night, and my friend had an older brother who supplied us, so we smoked and ate a whole bag of potato chips. It wasn't very exciting. I would smoke weed on and off until I was eighteen, when I had my heart broken and found it was the only thing that would numb the pain while I was at school. Smoking was just another way that I could be who I wanted to be.

One particularly boring Friday night, my friends and I decided to smoke weed in a closet in my parents' garage apartment. We all giggled, passing around a bong a friend of mine had bought. We tumbled out of the closet laughing, only to find my parents coming up the stairs. We sprayed body spray until it smelled like burned hair and hoped they wouldn't catch on. My mom walked up the stairs, and the first thing she said was, "I think something's burning up here!" My friends almost fell out of their chairs. I quickly blamed it on a faulty heater, and they went back to the house. Once they left, we erupted in a fit of giggles. The smell never did come out of our garage apartment. Times like this make it all seem harmless, but it wasn't. These isolated incidents seemed funny at the time, but it was never just about smoking or drinking; it was about running away from who I should be. When I was high or drunk, I hurt my family, ruined friendships, and lost people I cared about.

Most of the four years described in this book were spent running from the responsibility of being the person I knew I was supposed to be. I knew I should be a law-abiding citizen, a good daughter, a faithful friend. However, all I cared about was me and how and whether I fit in with the popular crowd. So I ran from that straight to who it felt good to be, and then I kept running. I was always running.

The cigarettes came along with everything else, just something to do to intensify the drinking. The first time I had one I threw up for hours. That should have been my first clue to stop, but of course I pushed through, until the nicotine was enough to calm my nerves after a long day of school. My three best friends and I all picked up smoking together until finally, when one girl's mom was diagnosed with lung cancer for the third time, we all vowed to quit.

A few years later that same friend's mom died from the habit we so carelessly picked up.

So these are the things that defined me—what I did and who I was with. It was all so harmless at first; I just wanted to fit in—and I did, but at what cost? What I gained was nothing compared to what I traded. I traded diamonds for dog food.

CHAPTER 2

GOOD-BYE, GOD

IN MY HIGH school days, my feelings ruled me. They were tied to every decision I made. If I felt lonely, I found someone to love me for a moment. If I needed a friend, I found a drinking buddy. If my heart was broken, I found a way to numb the pain. If I was lost, I asked my friends to point me in the right direction. It all started with my need to be someone outside our family. I watched my brothers accomplish achievement after achievement, and I knew I couldn't do it. My younger brother was following the same path as my older ones, and everyone marveled at his sweet personality and strong faith even at a young age. I didn't have the beautiful voice or lovable personality like Kristian did. I didn't have the gift of athleticism or the strength to stand up for my morals like Taylor did. And I wasn't kind and giving like Brett was. From where I stood, there was nothing inside Christianity that I could do to make a name for myself.

I believed the only thing I had was the drive to be different and, according to the world, a decent body with a workable face. I decided that if I couldn't be just like the rest of my family, then I'd be the opposite of them and find my niche in being different. I truly believed this. Living in the shadow of three "perfect" brothers made it very difficult to feel like my own person, especially since I was right behind Taylor, the classic all-American boy. Taylor was the quarterback of the football team, homecoming king, and president of the Fellowship of Christian Athletes, and he and his girlfriend (now his wife) were voted class couple. There was no way I could be as amazing as Taylor, much less top him. So I decided to rebel, and the minute I had my first beer it gave me the difference I was craving. My brothers chose not to drink before they were twenty-one, and they stuck by their choice even though they had friends who drank. I took the other route. I embraced alcohol like I embraced most of life—full force and without fear. I lived by the saying "Often wrong but never in doubt." Drinking gave me standing in the popular crowd, and acceptance into that club made me feel special.

I found out quickly that rebelling was easier than I'd expected. Everyone wanted to get a Stanfill drunk, because for six years my older brothers had gone through high school and taken a stand against underage drinking. I was never accepted into the group because of who I was; I was accepted because of who I wasn't. I wasn't the "typical Stanfill," so I became the black sheep. I figured if I couldn't have the whitest coat, then I'd dye it black.

I learned early on that high school only rewards a small number of kids, and unless you're the best or worst at something, there isn't a whole lot of recognition in between. You're either the best on the team or just another guy on the team. You're either the fastest runner or just another track member. You're the smartest kid or just another one trying to graduate. You're the prettiest girl or you're trying to be her. You're the coolest guy or you're following him. In a group of about two thousand kids there are typically only about fifty who fit the description of "best," and the others are left wandering around, begging for someone to look their way.

I wasn't an athlete (despite being five foot ten, my height just made me awkward), and I was by no means the prettiest girl. I wasn't the smartest kid; I could barely wake up for class. I wasn't a leader; I was too insecure in who I was. I was an in-between, but I was determined not to be.

'Cause When You're Fifteen . . .

At fifteen, I'd never had a boyfriend, had never been kissed, and was not in the "popular" group. I had friends and a social life, and I was by no means at the bottom, but I wanted to be on the top. High school is a lonely place to be, constantly surrounded by competition and boys wanting all the wrong things. At fifteen you're almost lucky if you make it out alive.

I've never felt more lost than when I attended high school football games as a freshman. I had to be driven there by my parents, who went because my brother was the quarterback, and I'd meet my one best friend by the lollipop stand. We'd wander through the crowds looking for girls to talk to or older boys to look at. All the popular kids our age had one place they hung out, in the corner by the concession stand. Normally girls would be there with their boyfriends, sometimes older guys, and it always ended up with some couple being chanted into having their first kiss in front of everyone. They'd peck, and the tiny crowd would erupt in applause. I'd even heard of some girls going down to the practice field, behind the stadium, to make out with their boyfriends. I wasn't in this group, but I desperately wanted to be.

At fifteen, I started wanting to be a part of the crowd as badly as I wanted oxygen. I longed to stand among the cool kids—and not just because of who my brothers were.

I wanted to have a strong upperclassman hold my hand as I walked proudly around the stadium. Instead, I was left following my much prettier best friend, hoping no one noticed how insecure I was. I was shy and awkward, partly because I was so tall. I was terrified of any and all boys and turned a dark shade of red whenever one would talk to me.

All I was asking for at fifteen was to belong, to be loved, and to be a part of something. Deep down, I wanted to be loved, not for a night but for a lifetime. I wanted to be found beautiful because of who I was, not what I looked like. I wanted a community where I could be vulnerable, not just Friday-night friends. I wanted so much, and my Christian life seemed to provide me with so little. As a Christian I felt so out of the crowd; I felt like an outcast. All I wanted was to be a part of the group that mattered, the community marked by popular girls, hot boys, and wild parties. . . . It's what I thought community was, and it's what I longed for.

It Started Off Differently, Though. . . .

I started high school with my values intact, content to be the third in line of my four siblings and follow my older brothers' lead as outspoken Christians. I went to the Bible studies, attended church events, and didn't say the f-word. The problem was, that Christian life wasn't mine. I didn't have a faith that I really believed in, just a set of rules

I had to follow. I didn't have a relationship with the God I talked so adamantly about, just an understanding of who He was in other people's lives. For me, God was a trend I followed until I turned fifteen, and then, like skorts, He went out of style.

It's easy to give something up if you never put your whole heart into it. I made the decision to leave God like you would sign up for new classes: I weighed the pros and the cons, and with what little I actually knew about a relationship with God, I chose to say good-bye. In typical me fashion, I wrote Him a good-bye letter, letting Him know I wouldn't be needing His services anymore. I said good-bye because in the end the things that I so desperately wanted didn't seem to come with the Christian life. I didn't really know God, so I only cared about what He could give me. I didn't think He could give me community, love, or a place to belong. I ended up being so wrong.

A week after I decided to leave God, I had my first beer. People like to think the devil is idle, that we stumble into him like a person on the street, but he is waiting. First Peter 5:8 says, "Be self-controlled and alert. Your enemy the devil prowls around like a roaring lion looking for someone to devour." He saw my turn of heart, knew the blow it could be to my life, and he pounced good. A few girls from the crowd I was desperate to be a part of invited me to have my first drink with them. I was thrilled. My mom took me over for a sleepover, met the girl's mom, and left me. After having dinner with her family, we waited until everyone was asleep and found a beer—one of those big cans of Bud Light. I remember thinking it looked like urine and smelled like feet. I didn't care, though. I drank it, and we all giggled, feeling like we'd just pulled off something big. The next day I felt a huge sense of accomplishment; I'd achieved the goal of being different from my family.

The truth is, I wasn't really looking for beer; I was looking for something to define me. If I drank beer, I was different from my brothers. If I rebelled, I became my own person instead of standing in the shadows of my well-accomplished brothers. I didn't realize it at the time, but my attempts to be different just made me ordinary in another crowd. I wanted everything I believed a life without God would offer me—cool friends, a boyfriend, and a chance to really have fun. And I got them all. I had "cool" friends who cared more about their popularity than me, a broken heart, and so much fun that I didn't remember most of it.

Once You Pop You Can't Stop

My first beer was such an electrifying experience I started to crave it, not because of how beer made me feel but because of what drinking accomplished. I was making a name for myself, in high school standards, by becoming part of the popular crowd. For me there was nothing more refreshing than being a part of something so different from my family. I would do anything to climb the popularity ladder. I made friends, and when they weren't useful anymore, I made new ones. I threw parties at my house so that guys would come over, and then I got grounded for a month when Mom found a giant vomit stain outside the bathroom. (I figured at least the culprits had been headed in the right direction.) I lost my parents' trust, but it was a small price to pay for my new life. No matter what it cost me, I would make my way to the top. There was one promise I made myself when I started it all, though: I wouldn't have sex. I knew I wanted to wait until I was married.

When I first got caught drinking, my parents tried to jump into my life in any way they could. They did their best to have a relationship with me despite my efforts to hate them. They showed unconditional love even though my bad attitude filled our house.

Shortly after my parents first caught me drinking, when I was fifteen, my dad decided we needed to go to father-daughter camp at JH Ranch, a Christian camp known for its appeal to teens. He thought a little church camp might cure my rebellion. I was livid. I didn't want to go to church camp even though it was in California and my dad promised we'd have a good time. So I cried. I was so tired of my parents telling me I needed to change; couldn't they see how happy I was? Apparently not. We went anyway.

At the camp they made us have "the talk" about sex.

I was mortified. My dad, being the communicator he is, took it in stride and revealed to me something I never expected.

It was one of those moments when you realize your parents are mortal, when you see that they've made the same mistakes other people have made and they're just as much a part of this world as everyone else. It's a shattering moment in childhood, and it's also part of growing up, part of shifting focus away from your earthly parents and focusing on your eternal One. As a child, no matter how much I loved God, no matter how many times I sang "Jesus Loves Me," He didn't measure up to Mom and Dad. In a sense, I believed God must have learned to be good from my parents. I remember thinking that there could be no better father than my earthly father, so why look?

I can still see the path we were walking down, the trees towering above us to form a canopy. It was cool outside, and we were deep in conversation. I was telling my dad about my grand plans and my need for freedom. I told him I didn't fit into our family, that everyone was far too perfect. He laughed. "Perfect?" he said. "That's what you think? Tindell, let me tell you how our family started."

Then he told me the story that kicked him right off my pedestal.

My parents met the summer before their senior year in college; my mom watched my dad break up with his long-time girlfriend and went in for the kill (at least that's how my dad tells it). She said she was instantly drawn to him. He was tall and handsome and played football for Georgia Tech. She knew he loved the Lord and was known among his friends for his ability to have fun without alcohol. My dad says he wasn't interested in her; they were at a pool party, and my mom had mascara dripping down her face. His ears only perked up when he heard her say she had to get home so she could go to church in the morning. They began talking about Bible studies, and my mom invited him to the one she attended. He accepted. My dad walked away excited that he had found a Bible study, and my mom walked away excited she'd found her next boyfriend.

The way my dad tells it, he went to pick her up and hadn't thought twice about his outfit or combed his hair. He was going to Bible study. My mom, however, was going on a date. She'd changed a hundred times (I only imagine this because she does that now) and done her hair to perfection. When she answered the door, my dad was suddenly aware of his appearance; he smoothed his hair and went to tuck in his shirt. My mom is the definition of captivating, and I can picture my dad's face based on how he still looks at her today: jaw open, eyes wide, mesmerized by her beauty.

This is the part of the story I'd heard; I knew they fell in love and got married. I always thought it was kind of a short story, but who bothers with silly details when it's your parents? Then my dad revealed the second part I'd never known: two months into dating, my mom got pregnant (I'm hoping not at Bible study, but I never did ask about that part), and the next month they were married. Kristian was born six months later, and so the Stanfills began. Two years later Taylor was born. Two years after that I came along, and two years later there was Brett.

At that moment I decided I would wait to have sex. I knew my parents had had the strength to handle the situation, but my dad told me how hard it had been on their marriage. He told me how they'd had to fight through the problems young couples face at the same time they were learning to be parents. He told me they'd had to grow up much faster than they'd wanted to.

Despite my rebellion, my dad and I had a pretty good relationship. Even in the worst of times, we understood each other. He loved my brutal honesty, and I loved that I could be honest with him. There was only one time I actually deeply disappointed my dad, and it left an impression that will last a lifetime. But that comes later. . . .

Father-daughter camp was fairly successful, except for the new friend I made. At night we had cabin talks where we'd go around and discuss what we'd learned that day. True to form, I never held anything back. If I had learned nothing, I would say so. If I thought the day had sucked,

I told the leader it sucked. One of the first nights, all the girls were going around saying their biggest fears. They all had real spiritual fears, like they wouldn't accomplish God's work or they'd fall into temptation to sin. I was barely paying attention, and when it was my turn to answer, I blurted out my biggest fear: not getting married. Later that night, one of the girls came up to me and told me she wasn't into the whole "church camp" thing either, and we talked about how, when we got back to Atlanta, we'd go to a concert together and get drunk. A few weeks later, my new friend from church camp called. We went to see John Mayer and got plastered on the way there. I *think* the concert was good; I was too busy vomiting to notice.

My dad and I left church camp no worse for wear and possibly a little closer. It kills me now to look back at the sacrifices he made for me that week. All he wanted was to spend time with his daughter, and I treated him like he had the plague. We did bond some, but only because I glimpsed that most daughters weren't as lucky as I was. It still breaks my heart to think about one girl we met whose father had been in a bad accident and lost a lot of his brain function. She had to remind him to do everything down to the last little detail. The day we were all supposed to go horseback riding she forgot to remind him, and as our horses were trotting away he ran up with an expression of pure disappointment on his face. He looked like he had failed her. At that moment I thanked God for a dad who could be a dad. In times like these, I realized how truly lucky I was, but the moment was always too short. Reality and my need to be popular always came back full force, and I forgot my blessings a lot more easily than I remembered them.

As soon as I could, I picked up my life as if we'd never left. A few weeks after we came back, my parents caught me drinking again. Where I grew up, parents had this phone chain, and even if you didn't want to be in it, you still got weekly updates about whose kids were misbehaving. Well, a Stanfill drinking made it to the top of the gossip reel, and my parents quickly got a phone call to let them know I was dabbling in alcohol.

My dad sat me down to talk about my drinking problem. This happened every time I got caught for something, and I hated these talks. I knew what he was going to say, but this time I could tell he was really worried.

He looked at me and told me about the rapids.

The "rapids" became my dad's and my way of talking about how I navigated high school. He said I was going down the rapids, and he was watching from the shore. He said he could see the bigger picture, but I could only see right in front of me. He could see the pitfalls and the traps that I couldn't, because he'd been rafting before. He knew I was approaching small rapids, and if I kept drinking, the rapids would only get bigger. When he talked to me like this, I'd laugh and tell him that I wasn't going down any rapids; I was just living life to the fullest. I lived by the Dave Matthews Band song I loved: "Celebrate we will. 'Cause life is short but sweet for certain." I was just living, having a few drinks to find out who I was. It was no big deal. I tried to tell my dad this, but he looked at me with something I hadn't seen in his eyes before: worry.

The problem with living like life is short but sweet for certain is that life isn't that short, and the decisions you make last a lifetime. I wasn't living a song; I was living my life, and every step I took would stay with me forever. Each drink, each boy, each cigarette, each joint would never be erased, and that's what my dad was trying to tell me. He was trying to warn me that this was much bigger than a few beers. He knew the rapids better than I did. In hindsight, maybe he could have said more, but at the time I think he did the best he could.

I should note here that my father is a brilliant businessman, a family man, and an excellent father. He has the kind of confidence that made me believe he could handle it all. I never saw my dad worry before this. No matter what happened, he'd just fly through life laughing. He could make anyone laugh, especially me, and when we got on a roll, people tended to ignore us. Although you have to be vocal in a family of six, my dad and I are both unnaturally loud. We've always had a strong connection, so when my dad looked worried, I listened.

He said, "Tindell, right now it's just drinking, but then it will be drugs and sex, and I don't want to sit across this table four years from now and see regret in your face."

I didn't see it this way, though. I just wanted to be popular. I didn't want to ruin my life or make mistakes I would deeply regret, but I would also do anything to be a part of the crowd.

CHAPTER 3

GIVING IT ALL AWAY

MY MOM NEVER gave me "the talk" when I was growing up, so consequently I learned everything I needed to know about sex from listening to my smartest middle school friend and overhearing boys' conversations—all very reliable information. (Yeah, right.) Needless to say, sex was interesting to me, kind of like dissecting a rat: I didn't want to go near it, but I was curious about what was on the inside.

Part of my curiosity came from the Christian home I grew up in. My parents weren't shy at all, but for some reason sex was a subject they almost never broached with me except for telling me not to do it. That was no problem.

I never planned on it. I was going to wait until I was married, because that is what good Christian girls do—they fall in love, marry, have sex, and then have a bunch of kids. Right?

See, I never got the flip side of sex. I was never told why I shouldn't do it, just that it wasn't right until marriage. That's great for kids who follow the rules, but it's kind of useless for kids like me who are hell bent on breaking them. The idea of being told not to "do it" just heightened my curiosity. At fifteen I was okay with the idea of not having sex, because most of my friends weren't doing it and I'd never been in love. But that changed.

When I fell in love, the reasons to not have sex were unclear to me. This is when having "the talk" would have come in handy. My parents did most things right in parenting, but in the area of sex talks, I was lacking information. I needed to know what sex can do to an unmarried woman. I needed to know the emotional damage it causes to her heart. It would have been good to hear from my mom about her experiences, because while facts about STDs might scare kids out of bed for a little while, they won't work forever. One day you fall in love and you never imagine that the person you love could have an STD or even worse—that he might move on to someone else. I'd like to believe that if I'd known a little more about my mom's past, I might have made different decisions. I'd like to believe that truth might have pulled me back to reality.

Because that feeling of being in love isn't reality. Passion isn't reality, and when it comes to sex, we all need a good dose of reality.

Even when I started drinking, I told myself I would make out and do whatever else my friends were doing, but I wouldn't have sex. I didn't want to have to tell my husband that I'd had sex with someone before him. This was the only value I promised to hold on to.

Let the Dating Begin. . . .

My first boyfriend was eighteen, and I was fifteen. I'd gone unnoticed at my school, and my best friend was dating a guy from another school, so in one supremely strategic decision I decided to date his best friend. I figured that way I'd get points for having a boyfriend and I'd still get to hang out with my best friend. A few of the "popular" girls had said he was hot, and even though he was an inch shorter than I was, I figured I'd give it a try.

Our dates mostly consisted of getting drunk at someone's house and making out for a while. He was older, though, and more experienced, and at some point making out wasn't enough. I don't remember when things changed. I just remember the pressure to make them change. People at school would ask me how far we were going, and I always alluded to things, but I was ashamed to say I had no desire to do anything else with him. He told me he loved me, and

I said it back because that's what you do when someone says, "I love you." It didn't feel like love, though—at least, not what I expected love to feel like. I never actually decided to let our relationship move past basic making out; I just got drunk enough that it didn't matter. My friends were all going further, so I figured why not.

I crossed a few lines without having sex, and then eventually I made out with another guy and let the boyfriend go. This was my trend for a while. Instead of having the messy breakup talk, I just cheated, and then the guys had to break up with me. I was careless with other people's hearts, because even though I said the words *I love you* quite often, I never really meant it. I cheated because I didn't know how to treat other people, and when I got drunk and my boyfriend wasn't around, I got bored. I cared far too much about whether or not boys wanted me, and one boy wanting me was never enough. I received validation that I was pretty through attention from boys, so it didn't matter who I was "committed" to. If another boy wanted to say the right things, he could have me—up to a point.

My first boyfriend was one of a few who were no big deal; I was fifteen and really just needed someone to drive me around. My relationships never lasted long, and I was never really interested in anything more than hanging out with my friends. My parents thought they could rest easy; since I wasn't in love, they didn't have to worry about me having sex.

♥

I made it through sixteen relatively unscathed by boys. My brother Taylor was now a senior and kept pretty good tabs on me. He had come to terms with the choices I was making and was more concerned about my safety than stopping me from drinking, which he knew he couldn't do. He told me that if I ever needed him, he would pick me up without question. Like the rest of my family, he was more concerned about not pushing me away with opinions. Kristian was in college, and I missed him like crazy, but I enjoyed the weekends when I could go visit him. Brett was in middle school, and my biggest fear was that he would start going down a bad path like me. But for the most part, my life was relatively smooth. All my parents could do was ground me and pray they'd get through to me one day. Everything changed, though, when I turned seventeen.

Like in all tragic love stories, I met a boy who wasn't like the others. We had a class together, but I have no memory of why we started dating except that he flirted with me during class. I flirted back. One night when I got drunk, I decided to kiss him. If the start was any indication of the finish, I should have known it was headed for disaster. We both made out with other people but realized after a while that we wanted to become "a real couple," so we decided to be exclusive.

It was all wrong from the beginning. He was a "leader of the pack" type. He had aggression issues and would fight just about anyone. We fell in love the high school way, with so much passion that our love for each other was equal only to our hate for each other. We'd spend the week screaming at each other on the phone and the weekends making out—behind closed doors.

I fell hard but still planned to stick to my last value: that I wouldn't have sex until I was married. He'd already had sex, though, and part of me wanted to be that connected to him. I believed he would never love me like he'd loved the girl he'd slept with if we didn't have that same connection. And part of me believed that if I loved him, I should give myself to him. He never said this; he didn't even pressure me. *I* pressured me. I pressured myself for the classic reasons that everyone says not to believe. All my friends were having sex with their boyfriends, and I started to believe it wasn't the big deal I'd made it. We were doing everything besides having sex, so what would really change? Mostly, I just wanted to be loved. I pressured myself, because I didn't think I was worth waiting for. I believed all the lies.

My commitment not to have sex until marriage was made two years before I fell in love. Since I was always more concerned with having fun than with having a boyfriend, and since I had a tendency to make out with anyone who was around when I got really drunk, my relationships never lasted more than a few months. (Think Kelly Clarkson's "Miss Independent.") Hear this: I had every intention of keeping my virginity fully intact, but when you've abandoned so many of your long-held principles, it's hard to remember why you should keep the last one. This is why teens crave internal boundaries: because these boundaries create a way to navigate through tough times. I didn't have boundaries, though. My motto was "Anything goes," and I lived my life in that manner. It didn't matter what my parents thought or what anyone who really loved me thought; I lived my life for me and no one else.

My parents had an inkling that my relationship was heading in this direction. My dad started to talk to me about making better decisions and realizing that my actions would have consequences. I didn't believe in consequences, though, because the only consequences I had faced so far had come from my parents, and to me they were enemies. I believed that if my parents would just leave me alone and let me live my life, then I would be consequence free and happy. Luckily for me, they wouldn't. They refused to take the easy route and stick their heads in the sand. They refused to brush off my rebellion as a part of growing up, and instead showed an intense love for me despite my hatred—a Christlike love.

My mom saw the classic signs that I was in love, and because she taught abstinence classes at the time, she told me lots of statistics about sex. But statistics didn't mean anything to me. I didn't care if most teen girls lost their virginity in their boyfriends' basements. Knowing that didn't stop my deep desire; it only gave me knowledge that had no effect on my behavior. My mom was great at telling me the reasons sex was wrong, but not great at telling me why sex was made for marriage. In classes, she taught the biological part of sex but not the feeling part of sex, and I lived my life based on my feelings. Statistics were her way of trying to caution me, but cold facts didn't change anything for me. My friends would laugh and say that obviously my mom's teaching made no impact—we'd all been through the same class together and it hadn't convinced any of us to be abstinent.

Looking back, I think what could have changed something for me was my mother's own story of heartbreak. What might have changed me was hearing that we're all tempted, that desire is real, that young love is powerful. But by this time I was already on the express train headed for disaster.

I started to wrestle with the idea of sleeping with my boyfriend, and I went to the only person I could talk to about my issues: my sister-in-law, Kerri. She sat with me in Starbucks and begged me not to do this. She told me story after story of people getting hurt because they had sex before marriage. She used logic and reason, and she left religion out of it, so I listened. But my heart was hardening to the idea of waiting. She told me later that there was something different in my eyes that day, like the life had been drained from me. I remember feeling just that, stuck at a crossroads with no real guidance. I was begging for direction, but I wanted to be happy—and wouldn't this make me happy?

The truth is, this relationship was different from any I'd been in before. I fell harder than I thought I could and suddenly couldn't remember why I didn't want to have sex. The idea seemed even better when I was drinking, which was most nights. I'd get drunk and forget why I'd promised myself to wait. Two months into our relationship, we were "in love" and crossing physical boundaries I thought I'd never cross outside marriage. Suddenly my commitment to wait until marriage felt really far away, and this opportunity was right in front of me.

Sin often involves yielding to a temptation of the senses. It promises instant gratification if you trade in long-term satisfaction. I could feel good right away if I traded in a marriage of purity. I tried to convince myself it wasn't that big a deal. And when I was drunk, which was often, it felt like something I really wanted. I knew we wouldn't get married, but I also knew what I felt was very real. I knew he really cared about me, and I really cared about him. When we were together, I felt like I was a part of something bigger than myself. I felt like this stage of our lives would never end, that high school would just melt into college and that we'd all be friends forever. I didn't let myself think past tomorrow or the next day. I loved fighting with him almost as much as I loved making up with him, because it showed me someone wanted to fight for me. I was on cloud nine when we were together, and it didn't matter what my parents or anyone else thought. I could see he wasn't the best choice. I could see we weren't meant for forever, but the now felt so good.

If you're there right now, I'm pleading with you to listen to my story carefully, because I didn't listen when people told me how much this would change my life.

It was one drunken night in his basement (every parent's nightmare), and I decided to give in. I didn't plan on it; I just got tired of fighting it. After we had sex, I left in a puddle of tears and called my three best friends for help. I'd broken a deep promise to myself, and I needed support.

They met me at my house, where we sat in my room and exchanged stories of how we lost our virginity, and we cried. None of us claimed to be Christians, but we all knew we'd lost something valuable. We cried for our futures and for what we thought we deserved. We cried because something inside us told us we were worth more than bad decisions in dingy basements. We cried because when sex isn't kept in the right context, it leaves you feeling empty and insecure. We cried because we no longer had a reason to believe we were worth more than sex outside of marriage. We cried because sex wasn't the fairy tale we'd thought it would be. It wasn't like the movies where it transports you to someplace amazing and then everyone parts ways and lives happily ever after. Sex was emotional and messy. It never left a clean break; instead it ripped us apart and left jagged edges that the next great love had to mend.

I went to church the next day with my family, something that was required, and it was the first time I remember feeling numb in church. The music didn't make my heart stir. Normally, no matter where I was with God, the music always called at something in me that begged for freedom. Beth Moore says, "Music is the expression of a freed soul," and my soul wanted to be free. That day, though, my soul felt chained to this world. I listened with a sense of heaviness, and when the service was over, I said I was sick and went home crying.

After I got over the initial shock of losing my virginity, I wanted to feel that closeness again, so I continued to have sex with my boyfriend. To be honest, sometimes I did feel close to him. This is the truth that adults are afraid to tell you. Here's the other part of that truth, though—the feeling doesn't last. The emptiness that follows does. Even though I loved my boyfriend, even though I could get lost in the moment, my heart kept telling me I was made for something greater. Even at a young age, I knew I was designed for intimacy to go with commitment. This is why sex outside of marriage left me insecure, because without commitment to back up the gift of intimacy, I had a chance of getting deeply hurt. I had a choice to make. Would I stay in this relationship, or would I break up with my boyfriend, make a new commitment to abstain, and move on?

I wish I could tell you that I moved on, but I didn't. I was so lost in my guilt that I didn't want to be alone along with everything else. So I kept drinking and having sex, and we had an on-again, off-again relationship. I had to drink to have sex, because I was so insecure in my decisions. I felt so ridden with guilt, and drinking made me forget about the guilt. My boyfriend was "experienced" and I wasn't, so I drank to feel the freedom to have sex. I drank because my body wanted what my heart knew was wrong. It still felt wrong, but my boyfriend never seemed to think so. I drank to forget that this wasn't how it was supposed to be and because I was scared that if I didn't have sex with him he would go somewhere else for it. He would often brag about our sex life in front of his friends, and I was so ashamed. I would ask him to stop, but to him it wasn't a big deal. We were having sex, but so was everyone else. I didn't have a moral compass to explain why it was a big deal, but it just felt like it was. It felt like a huge deal, and so I'd break off the relationship, and then when my heart would tear apart, I'd come back to him to mend it. I didn't realize that something that was just a physical thing could have such emotional and spiritual repercussions.

Our relationship was rocky before we had sex, but now

we had something new to fight about. We were always fighting and making up. No matter how bad we were for each other, we were connected, and I couldn't seem to make a clean break. Then, after a year of being together on and off, I made a decision that ended everything. I did what I always did and drank too much and made out with another guy. I woke up hungover, confused, and with a familiar guilt. After my friends told me what happened, I convinced myself that I could hide it from him, but in high school you can't hide anything.

When I saw him the next day, I acted as if life was normal and he'd never know. Secretly though, I knew I was spending my last days with him. On our last night together we went to a basketball game and then to his house afterward. I got drunk and we had sex, and it was my way of saying good-bye. The next day he found out.

I was at lunch with my dad; he had taken me out to talk about my drinking problem. The past few times he'd seen me, he'd smelled the vodka on my breath, and he was out of ideas. Midconversation, my boyfriend called screaming at me. He had heard from friends that I had cheated. He told me it was over and hung up. I walked back inside the restaurant and told my dad what happened, and he told me to go, that my decisions had taught me the lesson he never could. I called in sick to work and went to my best friend's house for comfort. I cried for hours and called my now ex-boyfriend until I gave up.

That night I came home and saw that my parents had bought me a dozen roses to let me know how much they still deeply loved me. I tried to thank them, but I felt so dead inside. I put the flowers in a vase by my bed, a reminder that my parents' love was all I had left.

That night I put on the Keith Urban song "Tonight I Wanna Cry" and let it repeat over and over while I sobbed into my pillow. Keith knew what I was going through. The chorus sang over me as I felt each piece of my heart shatter. "Alone in this house again tonight . . . pictures of you and I on the walls around me. The way that it was and could have been surrounds me. I'll never get over you walking away." I don't have to look up the words to that song, because they're imprinted on my heart. A break like that will leave a mark, and the sound track that plays while you shatter will always be there. So that song stays there, a quiet reminder that what I went through was real and that despite everything, the God who saved me is alive and well. I have to believe God thinks of this song when He remembers that dark time in my life too. We all have memories that are played to music, songs that can take us back so far that we have to work hard to return to the here and now. My sound track from that time is filled with sorrow, song after song that reflected my heart's pain.

It's so sad, so painful, but it's where I was then. I didn't experience a lot of joy, just heartbreak after heartbreak that I brought on myself. See, I was the one pressing play.

I chose the album, picked the songs, and let them play. I drank until I didn't remember making the mistakes. I gave myself away like I was something you get out of a vending machine, and so the sad songs played on. I didn't know how life could be any different. I didn't realize there could be a life outside the pain I was drowning in. I could have had joy. I could have smiled, if I'd only given up the things I thought were making me happy. I thought alcohol was making me happy. I thought sex was making me happy. They weren't, though. They were just things I did to kill the pain of being unhappy and the pain of losing someone I believed I really loved. It's a gut-wrenching feeling when someone tells you they'll fight for you and then they walk away. It left me questioning a lot, but mainly my worth.

I wish I could adequately describe the pain that followed my boyfriend leaving, but I can't find the words. I can only say that heartache has its name for a reason. I don't ache for him today, but I do ache to have that part of my heart back. I remember feeling chest pain, like a part of my heart had literally been ripped out. I felt broken, not spiritually but physically. Each day I was forced to look at him, knowing he had my heart. I couldn't blame it all on him; I'd willingly given it to him.

Since he was the leader of the pack, I was declared off limits. If he couldn't have me, no one would. At school I would hear guys yelling, "Whore," after me as I walked down the halls. I did my best to keep my head held high, but it was all I could do to get up in the morning. Only a few things got me out of bed: my family and friends, and drugs and alcohol. I relied heavily on alcohol and marijuana to kill the pain in the months that followed the breakup. My friends were there for me as much as they could be, but they couldn't stay with me at night. My family was great to me even though I didn't deserve it. And even though she didn't tell me at that time, my mom had a hunch about the nightmare I was going through.

At first, I was banned from parties, because my former boyfriend told everyone he couldn't be around me. So I was forced to stay home while my friends went out and kept me updated on his weekly escapades. To "get over me," he made out with a lot of my friends, and I was left at home mourning the loss of him and my social life. Each time I heard about another girl he was with, my heart would break a little bit more. I didn't understand why he couldn't just forgive me, but his pride was stronger than his love for me.

One particularly bad night he called me screaming that I was a slut, and how dare I think I could go to the school winter dance. He told me all the things I prayed weren't true about myself. I'd always hoped I wasn't the kind of girl that guys screamed obscenities at, but I took it; I believed every word he said. I got off the phone in tears and found a bottle of sleeping pills; I took ten and prayed I wouldn't wake up. When I woke up the next day, I heard a small voice telling me, "This too shall pass."

Knowing it was going to pass wasn't enough to heal the wound. The pain felt as real as the love did and was overwhelming. I was living my own nightmare, and each morning for months I would cry in the shower, begging that this day wouldn't be the same as the last. The only thing that kept my head held high was the encouragement my parents had given me earlier in life. Even though it didn't stop me from making huge mistakes, it came back to me later. Somehow, they did a great job of making me believe that I was worthy of love and respect. So while I wasn't being loved by a boy and I was constantly being disrespected, my parents' voices were still in my head saying this wasn't who I was. The life I was living shouted to anyone listening that I didn't think I was worth anything at that moment, while deep down in my heart a voice whispered that one day someone would love me for who I was and not for what I could give him.

Sometimes it was so bad that each breath felt like glass shards digging into my lungs. I fell into a pit so deep I couldn't see the opening. I tried desperately to get out of it, to take control, but the more I tried to take control, the bigger mistakes I seemed to make. This is when I began smoking weed before school. I loved seeing my former boyfriend because it was my only way to be close to him, but it hurt so bad I needed something to numb the pain. My best friend was going through similar heartache, so a few days a week we'd meet at seven in the morning and get high with a few guys in our grade. It helped temporarily, but the hours would pass and so would the high, and life was still the same.

I wrote in my journal about the pain I was experiencing, putting on paper the feelings I didn't want anyone else to know:

> *I tell everyone that I'm over him. I even praise him for leaving me alone to heal. I say he did me a favor by speeding up the inevitable, and part of me believes all this. However, in the back of my mind he is still an ever-present voice speaking his familiar words of love. I've even moved on to better things, even a better guy, but behind every smile I hide my insecurity that I'll never heal. I know he still has a grasp on part of my heart, and my mind wonders if he will ever let go. I don't need him and I don't even want him, but what I want is for us to move on and for him to let go. I want life to realign into a normal pattern where my mind doesn't race every time he is near. I care about what's ahead far more than I care about the past, but it's hard to walk forward when you can't stop looking back.*

Eventually, I started dating again. It looked like I'd moved on, but because the previous guy still had a part of me, I couldn't move forward. I couldn't let go even though I was ready to. I'm sad to say that it took years to let go of him, and the only way I eventually succeeded was by letting God repair my broken heart with His healthy one. Here's another entry, which I wrote three months and two boyfriends later, still clinging to the one who left:

Just when I think I have let him go, I stumble over an old picture or a song comes on, and my heart cringes. Then the moment passes. It hurts, but I'm learning to live with it. The pain never fully goes away, but I'm learning to live with the thorn that is his memory. He has become like a splinter stuck deep inside my heart, and I can feel the sting, but I can't remove it. So I cope. Even when I find myself in someone else's arms, the reminder of his presence stays with me. I can't recall a day free of him in almost two years, and while my life is moving, I seem to stay in his gaze, still keeping a tiny memory of us somewhere deep inside. When the pain gets so bad I can't bear it any longer, I let my heart dwell on him for a little while. I relive each kiss, each late-night talk, each party, and when I think I can't bear it anymore, when I think my heart will break, I make myself come back. I force myself back to the present time and cry for my empty arms.

Another month later . . .

I wonder if you can really love if a part of your heart is missing. Mine aches every day for the one it lost, and I would give anything to take him back. Tears fill my eyes at just the thought of him. At least I can say I have loved.

I used to love the saying "It is better to have loved and lost than to have never loved at all." After loving and losing too many to count, I know that saying is garbage. Don't love until you find a man who is worthy of it. Don't lose a part of you that can never be returned. It took years to get over my high school love. Our relationship wasn't even built on anything solid, mostly empty stuff like parties and drunken sex. We cared about filling a void for each other, and in our own messed-up way we loved each other, but I wish I'd loved myself enough to say no. I wish I'd had the strength to be different.

I remember one night before a party at his house, my best friends and I sat outside and took shots while we listened to "Just So You Know" by Pete Schmidt. The four of us had coined it as our song, and so we put it on and passed our handle of vodka around until we were drunk enough to forget whatever was going on in our lives. This was the first time I'd been allowed back at his house, and I didn't have the courage to see him and his new girlfriend—.

one of my "friends." So we drank and sang at the top of our lungs, each trying to drown our different pain.

When we finally made it inside, I watched as he did all the familiar things but with a different girl. My friends and I ended up getting really drunk and spraying everyone with a water hose to deflect the tension. He ended up kicking us out. As we all said good-bye, I watched as she stayed behind. Same moves, different girl. Part of me wanted to warn her that she wouldn't leave this relationship whole.

For the next few months I sulked around the house, and everyone felt the weight of my sadness. It was only my little brother and me at home, so the attention was mainly on me. My parents were at a loss for what to do. They didn't ground me, but they warned me that my behavior would only make the situation worse. They genuinely felt bad for me, but there was nothing they could do. I'd slipped down the rapids, and now I was dealing with consequences I'd created.

One night my mom asked the question I didn't want to answer: Did you have sex with him? The tears streaming down my face answered her greatest fear. I sank into her arms, not saying a word, letting the quiet sounds of my sobs speak for me. She brushed my hair with her hands like she did when I was a child, and for a few minutes life wasn't falling apart. She offered no advice, no reprimands, no I told you sos. Just love. She let it pour from her heart into my broken one, and the rift that was between us sank away for a moment.

I sat and cried in her arms for what felt like hours, and when I finally looked up, the only thing she said was exactly what I needed to hear: "I understand." It was the hope I needed to be able to continue. She had lived past this, so maybe I could too. She'd married a man who loved her, despite their mistakes, so maybe I could too. If she'd made her way out of this thing alive, maybe I could too.

> *Tears come streaming down your face*
> *When you lose something you can't replace.*
> —COLDPLAY

Fifty Bucks and a Case of Beer

There was a major question I wanted answered when I started sleeping with my boyfriend. I wanted to know what I was worth. More than that, I wanted to know if I was worth loving.

One of my favorite movies is *Almost Famous*. It's partly based on the true story of a journalist who goes on the road with a rock 'n' roll band and falls in love with one of the band's groupies, Penny Lane. Penny loves the lead guitarist, Russell, who is in a relationship but also uses groupies. Penny goes on tour with the band and lives in the fantasy that the tour will never end, and she believes Russell loves her. Meanwhile, the good-guy journalist, William, is falling for Penny. The tour is coming to a close, and they're about to go to New York, where Russell's real lover will be meeting them. At one point, Russell is gambling with another band, and he wagers Penny Lane for fifty dollars and a case of beer. William is watching and leaves brokenhearted. He goes to talk to Penny, who tries to convince William that Russell loves her.

PENNY: YOU DON'T KNOW WHAT HE SAYS TO ME BEHIND CLOSED DOORS. MAYBE IT IS LOVE, AS MUCH AS IT CAN BE, FOR SOMEBODY. . . .

WILLIAM: SOMEBODY WHO SOLD YOU TO HUMBLE PIE [THE OTHER GROUP] FOR FIFTY BUCKS AND A CASE OF BEER! I WAS THERE! I WAS THERE! LOOK—I'M SORRY.

PENNY: WHAT KIND OF BEER?

The first time I watched this I realized we've all been some form of Penny Lane, or at least I have. I had a price. It might not have been fifty bucks and a case of beer, but I had price. I was fooled into believing my boyfriend loved me, that he would fight for me, and that he believed I was worth a lot more, but the truth was I gave myself to him for a much lower price. He said the right things, made me feel the right way, so I gave in. I thought it was love, but the minute I made a mistake he was gone. Like

Penny Lane, I told myself that sex can be the basis of love and that what we had was love "as much as it could be." Just like Penny, I ended up in tears believing I wasn't worth anything more.

Penny Lane could be any girl, someone who fell in love and fooled herself into believing that when push came to shove, the man she was having sex with would pay the price for her. But why would he? She'd already given herself for much less. I gave myself for much less. I wanted love, so I traded myself for something that felt like love, and then when another offer came along, he traded me. I made out with other guys because I was insecure in who I was and insecure about what others thought of me. I cheated because when you get drunk enough, your morals don't matter. Mostly though, I cheated because I didn't care about anyone more than myself and making myself feel good. Because we didn't have the foundation of commitment to make it work, he left. I'm not justifying my actions, but I can promise you that if we were married, it wouldn't have been that easy. Walking away is a lot easier than staying. Staying requires hard work and sacrifices, and walking away requires nothing more than somewhere to go. We never know what Russell said to Penny behind closed doors, but I bet it wasn't much different than what I was told. Words are cheap, but commitment is hard work. You deserve a relationship that is safe, one that doesn't leave you questioning your worth in this world.

The thing is, if you're in a relationship but you aren't committed to that person, then you're replaceable. I was replaceable. After a few months apart from me, the "love of my life" found a new love, and seeing them together the first time was so hard I went to my journal to let some of my feelings out:

> *That was supposed to be me, not her. I know I leave in a month and I won't care who he is with, but right now it hurts to know he cares about someone like he cared about me. I want to think I was unique. I want to think he didn't take everything I had and leave me with nothing but a broken heart. However, his promises were nothing more than words written on his tongue, easily forgotten and washed away. I thought what we had was real, but how real? I know everyone comes to the point where their old relationship breaks away and the new one ties strings around their heart, but do I even want that?*

Just like every other girl in love, I wanted to believe that what my boyfriend and I had was special. But when "love" is only built on feelings, it's always replaceable. I wanted to be unique, because something inside of me told me I was. Deep inside, I knew God made me different from other girls, but I needed someone to validate that. I wanted to be unique, because standing out from the crowd was just as important to me as being part of the crowd. My parents always affirmed that God created me uniquely, for a unique purpose, but this relationship left me feeling like one more in a long line of replaceable girls. When it ended, I felt used and no different from any other girl who'd been dumped, and this challenged my belief. If I was so different, then how could he treat me like just another girl? He confirmed my biggest fear, that I wasn't special.

What are you trading your love for? What have you fooled yourself into believing? Do you think he loves you, but your heart feels insecure? Do you think he'll never love someone like he loves you? Is he asking things of you that feel cheap and leave you empty? I don't care what life has told you in the past; you're worth more than fifty bucks and a case of beer.

I traded my values for what I thought was real love. It didn't last, though, and I was left living with the decisions that I had promised myself I wouldn't make.

CHAPTER 4

A DIFFERENT KIND OF AA: ADDICTED TO ATTENTION

LONELINESS WAS A feeling that seemed to follow me through the halls of my high school. Even when I became part of the popular crowd, I would write in my journal that although I was surrounded by people I still felt all alone. I would drink to cure the loneliness and wind up more lonely than before. I was never really a casual drinker, more like a line-up-the-shots kind of girl, and after six or seven I would wander around looking for someone to hang on.

My friends joked that I got clingy when I was drunk, often hanging over whatever boyfriend I had at the time. I wasn't like this when I was sober. When I was sober, I was normally moody and disconnected. But when I drank, I smiled that sloppy vodka smile and hung on everyone I saw. When I was sober, I was angry, desolate, and hurting, but I couldn't show anyone that, because in terms of high school I had it all.

I was finally deemed pretty, popular, and cool, and although it was everything I had wanted, it didn't matter. The pain was greater. The pain of heartache and broken promises was a biting reminder that the life I'd invested my soul in was a lost cause. I'd given up everything that mattered—my family, my faith, and my body—to chase after this life, so I drank to get a good buzz and become who everyone expected me to be.

After I lost my first love, I tried to move on. I found someone new to love, and I fell faster than I thought I would. But then spring break came, and he told me he wanted to be able to make out with other girls, so he broke up with me. Heartbroken again, I turned back to my first love and tried to get love in the only way I thought I could: sex.

Sometime Senior Year

After months of silence, he decided we could talk. I was so relieved. I still hadn't gotten over losing my virginity to him, and I'd do anything for him to hear me out.

We'd been talking for the past couple of days, unable to break the chains of our old relationship. He told me how much he missed me and that it wasn't supposed to have ended how it did. I just kept apologizing, hoping he'd find the strength to put me before his pride. My best friend had a class with him and had been working to convince him that he should put the cheating thing behind him, that we belonged together. I didn't know if that was true, but I knew that I didn't want to be alone.

It was a Wednesday night, and my parents had a Bible study at church. My best friend and I planned to get drunk in my garage apartment. She brought over a water bottle of vodka, and we went shot for shot while we listened to Tim McGraw's "Live Like You Were Dying." It was our new favorite song, and it hit especially close to home since her mom had just been diagnosed *again* with cancer. We never talked about stuff like that, though. We weren't good with handling our feelings; they had too much truth in them. So we got drunk and talked about how stupid boys were.

I decided to text my old boyfriend and invite him over. I promised I'd sleep with him if he'd just come and see me. A tiny voice in my heart told me it wouldn't work, but I drowned that voice in vodka until it slurred. My best friend left, telling me to call her as soon as he was gone. When he pulled up, he called me, and I met him outside. He gave me a deep kiss, tasting the vodka on my breath. He laughed; he knew I had to be drunk to have sex.

I expected him to tell me he still loved me, that he

forgave me, and that we could be together again. Instead
we had sex and he left. I called my friend in tears; I was
reliving the heartache all over again. She tried to make me
feel better, but nothing she said could mend my broken
heart. I waited for him to call or at least text me, but nothing happened. He didn't say anything to me until a party
the next Friday night, when he announced to our whole
group of friends that I'd given him "breakup sex."

This isn't how God planned for me to use my body or my
beauty, but I didn't know who else to turn to for love. I
didn't know who to take my broken heart to except for the
person who broke it. He wasn't any better at handling it,
though. He got what he wanted and left me with the pieces.

> But you trusted in your beauty and used the
> attention to give your body to anyone who asked.
> You lavished your love on anyone who passed
> by and your beauty became a part of many who
> did not deserve it. You took your clothes off
> and prostituted yourself. Such things should not
> happen, nor should they ever occur. You took the
> gifts I gave you, the things of you given by me,
> and you made for yourself male idols and gave
> them whatever they asked for. And you offered

every special thing you had to them, your heart
you placed before them.
 EZEKIEL 16:15-18 (MY PARAPHRASE)

I didn't understand that my body wasn't a tool I could
use to get love. Because I was so lonely, I would do anything to feel loved. I traded so much for moments of attention to ease my aching heart. My addiction to popularity
and boys led me to do things I will always regret.

God intended us to use our bodies to honor Him; it's
one of our greatest gifts, so in it lies one of our greatest weaknesses. If Satan can convince you that you aren't
worth being honored, if he can make you believe that
you're worth nothing more than a Friday-night hookup
or a dirty picture message, then he can convince you of so
much more.

Your body is tied to every decision you make, and your
heart is tied to everything you do to your body. If Satan,
the Tempter, can break your heart and fool you into believing you can take your body out of the equation, then he
can keep you brokenhearted and downtrodden with each
hookup you experience.

The truth is, you can't take your body out of the equation. I couldn't take my heart and my body and separate
them. My heart and my body are one, and who I gave my
heart to was tied to who I gave my body to. They were not
and never will be separate entities.

Defeated, used, and destroyed. That's how I felt each morning after a night of drinking and giving my body away. I don't know many girls who wake up from one-night stands, pat themselves on the back, and say, "Good job. I gave myself to Mr. Nobody, and now I feel so much better about who I am." Attention is like a drug. It feels great in the moment, but it never lasts and only leaves you wanting more.

> Do you not know that your body is a temple of
> the Holy Spirit, who is in you, whom you have
> received from God? You are not your own; you
> were bought at a price. Therefore honor God
> with your body.
>
> 1 CORINTHIANS 6:19-20

In high school I was addicted to attention. I loved being noticed. I wore clothes that sent this message loud and clear, and I was only happy with a Friday night if I ended up making out with someone. Every Saturday morning I would wake up and feel more alone than ever; a tiny, evil voice in my ear would tell me, "You didn't feel alone last night," and I couldn't deny it, because there was some truth in it. For that split second I hadn't felt alone, but the feeling never lasted. So I'd do it all over again. I was covering the huge hole in my heart, where God belonged, with one-night hookups. It was like putting a Band-Aid over a bullet wound; it covered the gaping hole, but soon the blood would flow and break through. I never gave guys what they wanted just for them; it was always mostly about me. I needed the attention. I needed to know I was worth looking at. The cycle was always the same: I used them or they used me; I got tired of them or they got tired of me. In the end one of us always left. I got so used to the pain that I didn't feel right unless someone was leaving me. There were a few that were different, a few that wanted to stick around, but I was in no position to be anyone's girl-friend. I was much better at being someone's Friday night.

The challenge with this attention deficiency is that it doesn't go away just because you become a Christian. You have to deliberately fill the void in your heart with God's definition of you. Even now, whenever I don't have my heart fully focused on the Lord, I find myself slipping back into my old ways, subtle signs that remind me how human I really am. I watch for a man's eyes to follow me as I walk, and I breathe a sigh of relief that I'm still found attrac-tive. I know it means nothing, just a chemical reaction, but if I'm not careful, those small looks will turn into my self-definition.

Today I'm happily married, but I'm still a flawed human ruled by my senses, which means I have to fill myself deeply with the Holy Spirit to fight what seems natural. As much as God has healed me, there still remains a scar that reminds me who I used to be, a tiny place that can fester if I don't keep the ointment of His Holy Spirit slathered on.

He is the only thing that can keep me from slipping back into the pit, and believe me, that pit is never far—just a hop, skip, and jump away from God's will. I read chapter 16 in Ezekiel, and I see my life played out like a novel. I read it and hear my story. More than that, I hear the breaking heart of a Father. I see God noticing my shame and tears, covering me when I beg Him, and then watching as I run back out and give my heart away again. He comes to me, placing His protection around me and sheltering me with His cloak, wiping away my shame with His blood. I take it off, though, when some silly boy catches my eye. I throw off the cloak of my King to run after my male idols. I run after them and offer anything they want, a desolate, desperate girl trying to get love where it can't be found. Read the words at the beginning of Ezekiel 16 and fill in the idol with whatever it might be for you. What keeps you from taking God's hand and letting Him fill you? What are you chasing after?

We tend to think of prostitution as something that happens on some distant street corner and doesn't affect us. However, prostitution could be seen as simply giving yourself in exchange for something else. You lose a little part of yourself with each transaction. But there's no amount of money that could be used to buy you. If there were, why would Jesus have hung on a cross? He wanted your heart. If getting your heart were that easy, why not pay for it and be done with it? Because your value is beyond any coin; it comes from the death of a God who came in human form. The only thing worth your heart is a sinless man dying on a cross. Next time some guy grabs you and gives you a sly wink, give him two pieces of a tree, three nails, a hammer, and a crown of thorns, and tell him to prove it—prove that he can pay the price it takes to get your heart.

It's All Downhill from Here

I never thought that sex would be the level-five rapids that would plunge me to near death. If sin is the killing of your spiritual soul, then my spirit had terminal cancer. I was dying inside, and the only thing that mattered was making myself feel good, even if it was temporary.

After my traumatic breakup, I didn't know how to be alone. I surrounded myself with people so I could drown out any voice pleading with me to see reality. Drinking went from a weekend event to an everyday need. My friends and I could always find something that needed to be celebrated or something we wanted to be distracted from. I went from smoking pot occasionally to needing it most days before school. The parties got larger, the drinks got bigger, and the hangovers were worse than ever. By the middle of senior year, I had a growing stomach ulcer and a need to be loved that was so large I was finding anyone to fill the void. I was reaching my end. Each day my will to live got a little smaller, and my need for drugs and alcohol got a little bigger. What was once social now became essential, and when I couldn't drink, I found my way into my mom's medicine cabinet, where she kept a small supply of sleeping pills for traveling and painkillers for when her migraines got unbearable.

My mom told me later that there were many nights she would come up and watch me breathe just to make sure I was still alive. I spent most of my time grounded, but whenever I managed to get out, I got so drunk that I'd spend hours throwing up.

Finally one day, after I'd spent the morning throwing up, my behavior had become so severe that my parents worried I had a death wish. My mom had spent most of that year on her knees in prayer. My youngest brother was just as well-behaved as my older two, but he was getting lost in the shuffle. My parents had to devote almost all their energy to keeping me alive, and I was ungrateful yet needy. At this point my dad realized traditional grounding wasn't working, so he decided to try a different tactic. When my parents caught me drinking and driving at three in the afternoon, they took my car and made me drive my brother's '86 Accord. That stopped me from drinking and driving, and it also taught me a lesson. Because I cared so much about my appearance, my parents knew

I would refuse to drive my brother's car—it was old and beat up, and there was no way I'd be caught behind the wheel. The only reason I was allowed to drive at all was because my mom was so sick she couldn't worry about getting me around.

Then the book *Blue Like Jazz,* a Christian memoir about Donald Miller's life and his journey to Christ, came out. My dad assigned it as reading, and to his surprise, I loved it. Miller's raw, honest approach made a big impact on me. After the first fifty pages, I told myself that if I made it out of this lifestyle alive, I'd write a book. My dad also gave me community work to do, made me spend time at home, tried to monitor what I was doing, and basically tried anything he and my mom could think of that would send a message about the decisions I was making. There was more he could have said, but in the end, he said enough to make me realize I was doing something wrong.

Unfortunately, it wasn't enough for me to change. In fact, the only reason I remotely listened to him was because we had a relationship before my rebellion started, and he continued to have a relationship with me through it. I think this is something that's hard for a lot of parents of teens to do. My dad was tough on me, but he'd still take time to be with me. He'd take me out to lunch or dinner just to show me that no matter what I was doing, he deeply loved me.

My parents were wonderful at showing me what Christlike love looks like. They were abundant in their love, yet thorough in their punishment. I was so far down my road at this point that I never questioned whether their beliefs could be relevant for my own life, but I also never questioned whether they loved me.

By then, I'd completely lost my way. I stopped caring at all about my values and started giving my body to anyone who would take it. Anyone who could make me feel loved for a minute could have me. I had a few sporadic boyfriends but no relationships that amounted to more than a few months and more breaking of my already shattered heart. The message I kept receiving was loud and clear, like a megaphone in my ear: "You're not worth loving." Each decision I made fed into the lie that I wasn't worth any more than this lifestyle. I wasn't worth a future or a family that loved me.

The problem was that the alcohol wore off, the high faded, and the loneliness came back. Each time, I was reminded of the decisions I'd made. My broken heart was still beating, still screaming to be loved, and the boy I thought could heal me had said his good-byes. I had nowhere left to turn. My friends had become my family, but most of them were in the same situation, if not a worse one. We had formed our friendships with the same ideals in mind: we didn't care what the rules were. Only now we were all paying the price. We tried to fix it, though. We had our weird ways of coping.

The community I had built to keep me from feeling

alone didn't ease the loneliness that I felt every day. My need for popularity had driven me to do things I couldn't take back, but my social status didn't provide my breaking heart with any comfort.

CHAPTER 5

DISASTER WITHOUT THE BEAUTIFUL

WHEN YOU'RE LIVING a destructive life, you get to the point where the end becomes so near you can feel it like cold wind on your face. I knew I was brushing up close with the end. The fork in the road was coming, and I could either change or choose to slip into a spiral so deep the only thing that would get me out was rehab or death. I realized this, and instead of facing change I tried to take control.

I was never obsessed with dieting, because I love food. Not healthy food. I love cupcakes, cookies, cakes, ice cream—really anything with sugar and butter. I thought working out consisted of walking up a long flight of stairs, and I never worried about bikini season. I should say that

I have the metabolism of an antelope with the body of a giraffe; it's all in the genes, so my weight was never a huge concern. When I did fall into the trap of dieting, it was more because all my friends did it and I didn't want to be left out. I complained about my body because that's what you do at sixteen, and I worked out because my friends and I were all members of the same gym.

Then I got my heart broken when my first real love left, and something inside me shifted. My world was spinning desperately out of control, and I'm a control person. I enjoy leadership positions, I love making decisions, and I'm not overwhelmed by crowds—but I couldn't control my life. This guy I'd given myself to had all the control. He was the leader of our dysfunctional pack, and he decided I wasn't allowed to go to our school's winter dance, I wasn't allowed at any of the parties, and I most certainly couldn't date. I was in a deep depression, watching this boy I loved run around with all my "friends" while I was left sitting at home.

So I stopped eating. This new obsession started the minute he broke up with me. Suddenly, all food became unappetizing. Then I began making a conscious effort to avoid food altogether. After a few days my jeans felt a little looser, although they were only a size 4 to begin with. I found that my food intake was one thing I still had control of. I couldn't control what my ex did or whether my friends would hang out with me, but I could control food. So I refused it and witnessed my parents' eyes fill with concern. I still worked out daily, and everyone watched as my weight continued to shrink. At my height, you can't really lose that much weight and have it go unnoticed. When my collarbone started to stick out, people began talking. The more people talked, the more I enjoyed it. I wanted my ex to know he had damaged me, and by this point I didn't care what the consequences were.

After a few months, maybe three, I started dating someone new, and he constantly praised how thin I was. I was weighing in at 120 pounds at five foot ten and loving all the attention. I drank the control with a shot of vodka and hoped things would be different now. Of course, I should have seen this as a sign of my unhappiness; I should have given in and told my parents the truth, which was that I needed help. But I kept trying to fill the void myself. Life didn't get any easier, though. Each time I tried to move on, my heart got broken again, and I didn't know how to put it back together.

A few months after I stopped eating, the doctors told me I had to put on weight. My friends were begging me to eat. They even took me out and bought me meals. I could see that I was becoming unhealthy, but I loved the power not eating gave me. On some level I was aware that if I kept controlling my food, it would become a beast I couldn't control. I knew girls who had full-blown eating disorders, and I didn't want to end up there. But I enjoyed the attention so much; I liked being noticed even if it was for the wrong reason. I didn't stop eating because I wanted to lose weight, but I liked hearing that I was skinny. See, when your life is spinning out of control, you'll desperately grasp whatever you can. This was my grasping, and it was so easy. All I had to do was starve myself.

During this time, my parents had me in counseling to try and help me see that my behavior was hurting me, but I was completely unreceptive to what the counselors had to say. The temperature in the Stanfill house was rising. The more I starved myself, the more frantic my parents became. At first they were concerned about my destructive choices, then terrified. Then after one incident, they were panicked.

It was a typical Friday night for me. I was onto yet another relationship, and even though I didn't really care about the guy, I couldn't be alone. I was at a friend's house drinking with my new crush when his ex-girlfriend showed up, and they disappeared to a bedroom upstairs. After that, I started drinking more and called my best guy friend, and he told me to come over. He was my run-to guy, and whenever I was lonely we'd end up making out. I drove about twenty minutes, drunk and lonely, to where he was. By the grace of God, I made it without hurting myself or anyone else. I told my friend what had happened, and we decided to split a water bottle full of vodka shot by shot. That's sixteen shots total, and I'd already had seven or eight. By the time we were halfway through the water bottle, I was out.

The next morning I woke up half-dressed and hungover, my cell phone ringing by the bed. It was my mom. I told her I was on my way home from the friend's house where I was supposed to be staying. I knew I smelled like vodka, so I sprayed some perfume I kept in the car and downed a bottle of water. I was still drunk. When I got home, my mom told me I needed to clean my room. She eyed me suspiciously and asked if I was okay. I lied and made it up the stairs before I passed out. Next thing I knew, she was waking me up. The room was spinning, and I ran to the bathroom and started throwing up.

The whole room filled with the stale smell of vodka as my mom watched me empty my stomach. It didn't stop. I threw up for the next hour or so, probably once for every shot. I tried to tell my mom I had the stomach flu, but she wasn't buying it. I spent the rest of the day in bed. My dad came home early, and I overheard their concerned voices in the hall talking about what to do next.

Back to the Rapids . . .

My dad sat across the table from me just like he had three years earlier, and he looked at me with the same worried face. I saw something I hadn't seen before: disappointment. Then he reminded me of the conversation we'd had three years ago, the one where I'd told him that drinking was just an experiment and that I was only having a bit of fun. I'd told him I was just enjoying high school. Three years later, he looked across the table and saw his little girl depressed and broken. My dabbling had drained the life out of me, and if you really looked into my eyes, you could see my soul was dead.

He said, "I tried to warn you where this was going." And with a slow shake of his head, he told me he'd tried to prevent this. I was drowning in the rapids, and he was afraid I was past the point of saving. I'd committed the sins, and now he couldn't help me. At fifteen I was just experimenting, but at eighteen I was drowning in my sin, soaked in the waters of depression and loneliness. In that first conversation he'd told me that if I kept going, I would have sex, I'd be doing drugs, and I'd be addicted to alcohol, and he was right. I was exactly where he knew the rapids would take me.

See, the details of your journey may be different, but the destination is always the same. Maybe your temporary high from the popular lifestyle will last longer than mine did, but it will always wear off. Eventually, reality will hit you in the face, and you'll find that this kind of life is empty, and the more you want for yourself the less you can really grasp.

As much as he wished he could take away my pain,

my father couldn't. He couldn't erase where I'd been, and now I would always carry it with me. Then he cried. I'd seen him cry only once before, at my great-grandfather's funeral. But on this day he cried. He cried for his lost daughter and for the pain of regret. He cried because there was nothing he could do. He cried because he believed in me and knew I was meant for better. He cried because he couldn't protect me like he had when I was a little girl, and he cried for my broken heart.

This seemed to be the beginning of the end. I'd gotten into Auburn University, but my parents told me if I didn't clean up my act then I wouldn't be going to Auburn in the fall. They grounded me indefinitely until they were certain I wasn't a danger to myself. I was already alone, and now I was caged. I didn't know what to do. I carefully considered suicide but realized I didn't have the guts. I wrote good-bye letters to my parents and then tore them up. I would sit in my room with a handful of pills and then change my mind. Somewhere in the pit of my stomach, I knew this wasn't the end. The quiet voice of God's Holy Spirit that I'd tried to drown in vodka was still alive and still trying to get my attention.

God never gave up on me. Even after I gave up on myself, He still had a plan for me. And despite my constant attempts to escape Him, He was all that remained. I came to the end of myself. I was heartbroken, desolate, and desperate. It was my senior year, and I was set to leave for Auburn that fall. I refused to do anything that would endanger that opportunity. I stayed grounded for a month or maybe longer before my parents decided to let me out.

While I was grounded, I got a few packages from old family friends saying that they were praying and that for some reason God had put me on their hearts. They sent prayer books that I wouldn't read, but the fact that they'd reached out to me meant something. I couldn't shake the idea that people I hadn't spoken to in years had reached out to me on behalf of God. So it began—tiny pinpricks to let me know even though I had abandoned God, He hadn't abandoned me.

At this stage, writing was my only solace. I could go to my journal and pour out my broken heart without being judged. I could show the page what I couldn't let anyone else see. This was my way of healing in these hard times. I had an outlet no one else could see, and like all creative endeavors, it freed my soul. For me, creativity was part of the healing process. I believe that getting my thoughts and feelings down on paper literally saved my life. I have one-too-many drafted suicide notes that were never acted on because just writing down my pain released enough hurt to let me go on. What I know now is that creativity is one of our most precious gifts. God is a very creative God. If you doubt that, just look outside or in the mirror. God is the Creator; therefore, He is ultimately creative. We were made in God's image; therefore, we were made to create. Whether it's in writing, drawing, music, or whatever else you love, it will be healing for you.

My oldest brother is a songwriter and singer, and he tells me he makes the best music whenever he goes through rough times. We can use our creative expression to free our souls, find our uniqueness, or praise our King, because we're made to create. So here was my voice during that time of my life:

When I look in the mirror, that face that stares back at me haunts my every nightmare and breathes life into my deepest fear. The face that stares back at me is one of lost dreams and empty promises. This is what threatens my being; the shadow in the mirror is one of no hope and broken love. The image is a daunting reminder that I'm forgotten and unappreciated by the people I thought loved me. My face is one of pain, and if you look into my eyes you can see rivers of sadness and mountains of brokenness. My demeanor brings darkness and alienation. You see no love and little compassion. If you look deep enough, you may view the scars that have been burned in my soul by lost lovers and friends who betrayed me, and if you can see past my rough exterior, you see a little girl who is dying to be loved. To get past the exterior is humanly impossible,

so I build walls of UN-trust and broken bridges of
hate, because after this I'll never love again.

My journal was the one place I could be me. When I was writing, I could shed my rough-and-tough exterior and let my dying soul out. I have pages and pages of pain, notebooks where I'm begging to be healed, to be loved, to be made whole. I didn't know how, though, so I just wrote what I really wanted to say to the world. I wrote all the pain that I bottled up every day. I was searching, always looking for something to complete me, so I fumbled around from one dark thing to the next, hoping something would satisfy. I kept hoping that maybe the next thing would make me happy. Sometimes, for a brief time, it did, but it never lasted.

But there was one thing left. One thing that could still get my attention: watching my oldest brother lead worship.

Good Friday

I promised my mom I would go with her to hear my brother at our church's Good Friday service as long as she would let me go to a party right afterward. I was suddenly regretting that decision as we pulled up to the church. It was already seven o'clock, and I knew most of my friends would be drunk without me. As we made our way into the candle-filled sanctuary, something came over me like a wave of relief. I could almost feel God in this place. I quickly pushed it out of my mind; God had no place in my life.

The stage was set up in the middle of the sanctuary with chairs surrounding it. I saw my brother playing the guitar by a wooden cross standing in the middle of the stage. We sat right in front of him, and I gave a tiny wave. He was the only reason I ever went to church; my pride in his talent outweighed my hatred of church.

Then he started to sing, and I tried to ignore the words as they washed over me.

> *Jesus paid it all,*
> *All to Him I owe;*
> *Sin had left a crimson stain,*
> *He washed it white as snow.*

I couldn't help but wonder if He, Jesus, could really wash my sin away. I knew my sin was more of a black cloak than a crimson stain, but for a second . . . I wondered. Slowly, a battle of questions began in my head.

Could Jesus set me free? Could He take this broken heart and fill it? Could He forgive the horrible things I did to my family and friends? What about drinking? Well, I had to drink; I didn't know how to be fun without it. More words I tried to ignore:

O praise the One who paid my debt
And raised this life up from the dead.

I knew I had a debt. I knew I had too much sin for one man to take on. I needed my own cross. I told myself that just like the boys I'd been with couldn't rescue me, Jesus could never help me.

I tried to stay strong and keep my thoughts on what I was doing after the service, but the quiet voice I'd been trying so hard to destroy came to life. My heart began to quicken, and I could almost feel forgiveness—I only had to ask. I didn't want it, though. I wasn't ready to change. Instead, I let the tears fill my eyes and overflow down my cheeks. I cried for my broken heart and for the shame of my sins. I cried because I knew I needed Jesus, but I wasn't ready to give in. I cried because I wanted to stay in this place forever, sheltered from the pain of the outside world, sheltered from yesterday's broken promises and tomorrow's failures. I cried because I wasn't strong enough to make the right choice.

My mom reached over and placed her hand in mine, a quiet reminder that she was there for me. I knew she was. I knew that one day I would cry because God had redeemed me. I knew one day my mom and I would be great friends.

There were many times like this, tiny reminders that God was still watching me. My mom would tell me she didn't feel good about something, and lo and behold, the cops would come to a party. Many times she would warn me against people or places, and she was always right. She knew when she needed to be on her knees in prayer and when to be peering into my bedroom to make sure I was still breathing. She knew because God hadn't given up on me. She called it her "mother's intuition," but my parents always knew that God was protecting me.

I left high school with big scars but no permanent damage. I think it was God's way of telling me He wasn't done with me.

CHAPTER 6

DESPERATE TO BELONG

IT'S NOW SIX years since I was in high school. I sit at Starbucks watching a high school girl with her friends. She takes a long drag on her cigarette and drops the f-bomb a few times as she talks about her latest breakup. She complains about how hard life is and all the drama she hates so much. It feels very familiar: the cigarettes, the f-bomb, but more important, the anger. There's always something to be upset about, because, let's be honest, life really isn't fair, especially when you're sixteen. As she lights up another cigarette and talks incessantly about herself, each word drips with disdain. I want to give her a hug (while putting out the cigarette) and tell her it will get better.

When I was going through high school, the greatest anger I felt was toward my family. They were a constant reminder of the Christian life I had given up, and I partly blamed them for my heartache. I was angry that they were so happy and that they didn't understand why I wanted to be different. When we'd go on long car trips, my parents would put on Andy Stanley sermons that I refused to listen to. I put on my headphones and turned up my favorite rap CD (very hard core, I know).

There were so many reasons for my anger. I was angry that life wasn't as easy as I wanted it to be; I was angry that my family didn't understand; and I was angry that I didn't fit into their perfect mold. Still, they loved me. When I was grounded and couldn't see my friends or have a social life, they remembered what it was like to be a teenager. They'd get me out of the house, maybe take me out to dinner. On the New Year's Eve after I'd had my heart broken, my mom brought me downstairs to hang out with all their friends. I still remember sitting with her in the dining room, her stroking my hair and laughing with her friends. She wanted me to know I wasn't alone. She wanted me to know that she still wanted me near. My parents always made me feel loved, even in the midst of punishment. I never doubted their love, but I desperately wanted them to understand why I needed my freedom.

The only thing I knew was to fight back against what felt so unfair. My mom and I had screaming matches where we both left crying and my dad had to pick up the pieces when he got home from a long day at work. When my parents went out of town, I had huge parties. My little brother would be locked upstairs, scared to come down. My oldest brother came home once to find all my friends drinking beer around the pool while I was at work.

Everyone in my family suffered. My brothers would try to talk to me, but I was as hardheaded as I was driven. I tried to make them understand that I wasn't hurting myself, but they weren't blind. I was the one who was blinded by my own need and blinded by what I thought I needed.

My friends all loved my family; my mom was even asked to coach our recreation league soccer team, the Hellions. We took smoke breaks in the middle of practice and showed up to all the games hungover. Mom loved us, though. She shook her head from the sidelines when one of my teammates got a red card for screaming and running full force at a player on the other team. My dad was equally loved; my friends would come over whenever they needed a good laugh, and most of them called him by his first name. All my friends were jealous of what looked like our normal, loving family, because a lot of them didn't have that. Most of my friends' parents were either divorced or didn't like each other. A few friends had parents who were alcoholics. They all told me how lucky I was, but I couldn't see it. I was convinced that my parents were the problem.

Honestly, I was just a brat sometimes. One year for spring break my dad went above and beyond and rented this amazing house with a pool, on a golf course, and he even let us take the rental car to get lunch and stuff. Somehow, on vacation on a tropical island, I found a way to whine and complain. Finally two of my best friends got on me; they could see how lucky I was, but somehow I couldn't. I ended up yelling at them about how they didn't understand what it was like living in a family so unlike me. This was partially true. I was living a very different life from my family, but I'd decided to change who I was. My family didn't make that decision. I expected them to change because I had, and when they didn't, I pitched a fit. When they wouldn't mold to my new beliefs, I became angry.

Because my mom was chronically ill, she had to rely on me a lot to do the things she couldn't. One afternoon she was in bed with a migraine and asked if I could pick up my little brother from church. I told her I would, even though I was drunk, but then I forgot and came home wasted with my best friend. She had to get out of bed with a severe migraine and a fever and go get my little brother. I was that selfish; it was always about my agenda and what I wanted.

There was one person I allowed in my tiny world: my sister-in-law. She met me at the height of my rebellion, and even though my brother Kristian warned her that I tended to say whatever I wanted, he didn't quite prepare her. We were all decorating the Christmas tree and drinking hot chocolate in a kind of picturesque moment, when my mom asked Kerri if she wanted to spend the night (which meant I would be sharing my room with her). I quickly responded without even thinking, "But Mom, we don't even know her!" This was the beginning of Kerri's and my relationship. She laughed it off and did stay the night.

My birthday was a month later, and even though I was so rude to her that night at my house, Kerri sent me a present, and I instantly liked her. From then on, she became my confidant, someone I could really talk to about life. Whenever I was going through something and needed someone to talk to, she was there. She was my go-to person, and there were so many times I called her crying. She probably got more than she bargained for when she married my brother, but she was a sister for better and worse. She slipped in Christian advice the best she could, but mostly she just listened to and loved me. She knew there weren't words powerful enough to pull me out of my pit, but she could listen. She could talk through things with me like no one else could. We'd meet at Starbucks, and I'd tell her about the latest mistakes I wanted to make. She'd listen, never interrupting, and then try to help me see the light. I often disregarded her advice, but it still stuck in the back of my head.

The journal that I filled with my stories was a birthday present from her and Kristian. I'm sure she often felt like her investment in my life was in vain, but she found out later how much it really meant to me:

I think she was angel sent. I had another bad day where death seemed like the only option and where life hurt so bad I could barely move. I was considering my situation when a quiet voice came from my door. She's not here a lot since her home is with my brother, and on a day like today she was just what I needed, a smiling face, and an understanding ear. One that didn't judge and only cared. It's been a while since someone has genuinely cared, but for her it's all in a day's work. She puts others first, and when your life seems to be in pieces, she helps you sort it out. Although she isn't blood related, I don't need a piece of paper to tell me she is my sister through and through. Tonight seemed like the end, but I know we have many late-night talks to come.

When I finally accepted Christ (more on that later), she was there, and we embraced, crying as sisters in Christ, finally united by something stronger than blood: eternity. All her work that seemed to fall on deaf ears for years was worth something. She never gave up on me. Thank the Lord, none of my family did.

My family did what only Christ can empower us to do: they loved me unconditionally. I never deserved my parents' love. In fact, I spat at their offer, but they still loved me. Don't get me wrong—they're human and they broke down every so often, but they always loved me, even when they didn't feel like it. What was even greater was they forgave me when I asked.

Then There Were My Friends. . . .

See, friendship is the booze they feed you. They want you to get drunk on feeling like you belong.
—*ALMOST FAMOUS*

When I was fifteen, I desperately wanted friendships with the "cool" girls. They all seemed so confident, and I wasn't. They were comfortable around guys, and I wasn't. They were offering so much, but I had so little to give back. Somehow I wiggled my way into the group, but it always felt like something I could lose in an instant. I had to be careful that I looked the part, acted the part, and embraced the part. It was exhausting. I was always worried someone was going to realize I was a fake. Mostly, I was worried that I'd screw something up and be kicked out of the crowd. I'd seen people come and go, and I was determined to stay where I was.

Because I was so scared of losing my spot on the social totem pole, I tried things a lot of other girls wouldn't just to impress them. I tried to say the right things so that girls didn't think I cared what they thought of me. I based all my decisions on being a part of this group. It didn't really matter in the long run, though; ten years later I'm only close with a select few—and not for any of the reasons we originally became friends.

By senior year I established a close-knit group in our popular group of twenty plus. There were four of us called the "Fun Four." We were known for our heavy drinking and ability to liven up any party. We did everything together. We rode to school together, had a spot in the hall where we met, and all worked at the same day care. We picked up the same habits and quit them at the same time. If one of us was in trouble, we helped her, and we always seemed to be in trouble. We were there for each other in the good times and in the bad, but we still had to be loyal to the rest of our big group. There was silent competition between everyone in the group, and I never knew who I could trust. The Fun Four formed because we weren't typical girls in many ways: we weren't prissy and didn't talk about our emotions a lot—and we were reckless. We bonded because of that. It was our place of solace in our dark world. To handle heartache, we drank; to handle loneliness, we called each other; and to handle life, we went to another party. We always knew we had each other. If only we could have saved each other.

By senior year, we developed a routine. We'd get high before school, go to almost all our classes, go to the gym, then have a cigarette on our way to work (we were clearly concerned about our health). Everywhere we went, we listened to depressing country music. We loved "depressing country," coining the phrase because we were always listening to songs about breaking up, leaving, or being cheated on. We would plug my iPod into the car and blare "Goodbye Time" while we talked about our latest heartache.

There was always enough heartache to go around; we were always screwing up relationships or fighting with our boyfriends or falling in love with someone new. That seemed to be the trend around the high school halls—so much heartbreak we didn't know where to take it, so we listened to how other people handled it. We just wanted to know we weren't alone in our feelings; we wanted to know that other people were hurting, and country music has great sound tracks for a broken heart. Sadly, that wasn't the worst, though. The older I became, the closer real tragedy seemed to get.

CHAPTER 7

DANCING WITH DEATH

SENIOR YEAR, SPRING break. A milestone for any high school kid, and all my friends were going on an all-inclusive trip to Mexico (the kind every parent dreads). However, my dad told me if I didn't go on the trip, he would take me and two of my best friends anywhere we wanted. We picked Aruba, partly because there was no drinking age and partly because we wanted to see the clear water and sandy shores. The three of us had a knack for getting into trouble, and when we first arrived, we ditched my parents and found a liquor store and bought the nastiest coconut rum I'd ever had. It tasted like Banana Boat and piña coladas all mixed into one, but it did the trick. While my parents and the rest of the family went golfing, we sat around the pool at the house my dad had rented and drank rum until we laughed at anything.

After a great dinner out, we decided to steal the rental car and go to one of the local clubs. We had no concept of danger, and at two o'clock in the morning, with everyone fast asleep, we drove the tiny Toyota Corolla to Carlos'n Charlie's. We'd heard it was the best club, and we were eager to enjoy the liberal drinking laws of Aruba. Right away, we made friends with all the bartenders and started dancing.

Around three, the bar was starting to close and I was lonely. My two friends were dancing with a small Mexican man, but being five foot ten, I was left standing in the corner. I heard a voice behind me ask if he could buy me a drink. When I turned around, I noticed right away that this man was different from the other guys in the bar. He wasn't from Aruba, and he definitely wasn't American. He was tall and kind of cute, and I was on the mend from a broken heart, so I figured, why not? We danced and ended up kissing. When I started to leave with my friends, he followed me out. He kept asking me if I wanted to leave with him, and I knew that wasn't happening. A kiss was fine, but leaving with a stranger was something not even I was dumb enough to do. He told me he'd find me tomorrow, and before he left I caught his name: Joran van der Sloot.

We went home thinking nothing of our newfound friend, and the next day he found us on the beach again.

Once I sobered up, something inside me told me he wasn't to be trusted. When he asked me if I would go out with him alone, I refused. Thank the Lord I did. He got my number and called and e-mailed me a few times, but I never responded. My friends asked me why I blew him off, and I told them something about him gave me the creeps.

A few months later my best friend called, screaming at me to turn on the news. I did, and there was the Aruba guy suspected in the disappearance of Natalee Holloway. I gulped. Suddenly life became a little clearer than it had been five minutes earlier. *This is not a game,* I thought. But that wasn't a thought I wanted to hear, so I tried to put the memory behind me. I wasn't proud of my lapse in judgment or how careless I'd been with my safety—just the opposite. I'd survived and I didn't know why.

The question that follows this story is always the same: Did I contact the police? The answer is no. Natalee's case had become so big I didn't think anything I could say would make a difference. It didn't occur to me that connections might matter, and I honestly didn't think I had any information that could have been useful. If I'd thought I had anything useful, I would have contacted them immediately. But as I watched the story unfold, I was ashamed. I was ashamed that I'd made out with him. Most of all, I was ashamed I'd lived to tell about it while Natalee's parents wondered what happened to her.

I don't know exactly why I didn't leave Carlos 'n Charlie's

with Joran van der Sloot when he asked me to. Maybe it was because I had two friends with me and I hadn't had enough tequila to completely silence my intuition. Or maybe all those years of "don't go home with strangers" talk finally took hold. Since I had to drive the rental car, I'd purposely drunk less than my friends. Getting a DUI would have been the end of my parents' grace and probably the end of what was still going to be a fun vacation. So I only had a few shots—for me that was nothing. I think that's one of the things that saved my life. Had I been drinking as heavily as I normally did, I might have left with him and not thought twice about it. But because I was slightly sober, something in me told me not to go.

Once the story came out, and my friends and I confirmed it was the same guy, I tried not to watch the news. My best friend followed the story incessantly, but I just couldn't. Every time I turned on the news it was a reminder that this could have been me. I could have been Natalee and not come home. So many feelings hit me in waves. What I clearly remember is that for a few months after the story broke, I was just happy to be alive.

Some time later, my dad was looking for a picture on the computer, and he saw a picture of Joran and me we'd taken at the club. He ran and grabbed my mom to show her. My mom took one look and burst into tears. Suddenly, she realized how close she'd been to losing me.

LIGHT

CHAPTER 8

IT FEELS LIKE HOME

I STILL REMEMBER the feeling of driving to Auburn, rental car packed to the brim with the last eighteen years of my life:

I nervously pick at my lip, a recent habit, and watch as we get farther from the place I've always called home. It's nervous excitement, or at least that's what I tell myself. It's time to start a new life, one where no one knows that the name Stanfill goes with Bible studies and Jesus freaks, a place where I can finally be me outside the shadow of my family.

Eighty-seven miles to go. My mom talks in a quick chatter like she always does when things are changing. My dad tries to make jokes about all the cow pastures we're passing, and I try to look like this isn't the biggest change I've ever made.

An hour ago, I said good-bye to two of my three best friends, both headed to different colleges. We aren't emotional girls, but this good-bye warranted tears. We cried and then made fun of each other for it. We hugged and promised things would be the same, but part of me knows they never will be. I watched as they pulled out of my driveway. They are as close to me as the sisters I never had, and I can't believe they won't be with me for this next phase of my life.

Forty miles to go. My mom is talking about dorm colors, and my dad's wondering if anyone will think he's in college. Sorority rush starts in a few days, and I pray that no one knows my reputation. I go over my outfits in my head, hoping no one bought the same J.Crew dress that I have. I know rush means I won't be able to party for a few days, but I think my roommate is bringing some wine to ease the pain of move-in. My thoughts wander on until we finally reach exit 51, which leads to my home for the next four years.

We pull into the dorm parking lot, where attendants direct us to the nearest parking spot. I wish we'd brought my mom's Lexus; it makes us look so much cooler than this ugly rental. I make a mental note to mention it's a rental to my new suitemates.

Thankfully, one of my best friends is also going to Auburn, and she'll be one of my roommates. I've decided this is a good thing. I hope that somehow she might help me become less of a drunk. I can finally see that the life I created for myself that revolved around what felt good, looked good, and gave me instant gratification was leaving me empty. Maybe with a new life I might feel the joy my heart so desperately wants.

I know my friend's already moved in, because I see her car parked in the lot where we stop. The moving process begins, one heavy box at a time. I don't like manual labor; it doesn't make me look good. Begrudgingly, I help my parents carry boxes up three flights of stairs, no elevator. The dorms are old and smell like sterile cleaner. My roommate is already unpacking, and I hug her and thank God I get to see a familiar face. The next few hours fly by, and before I know it our room has become a home. A tiny TV sits at the top of a big shelf, dressers are crammed with clothes, and a desk is full with computers and school supplies. This is the part I'm dreading: saying good-bye. I hate good-byes; they've never gone well for me.

I look at my mom, tears spilling from her eyes. I wrap her in a huge bear hug, the kind that says things will be okay. Despite our many differences (or should I say biting similarities?), I know I'll miss my mom deeply. She may not agree with my decisions, and I don't agree with her faith, but she's my mom, and that relationship binds us. She tells me she's so proud of me, and I can't think of any reasons why. We don't say a lot, just hold each other and hope this isn't really good-bye. More tears brim in her eyes, and I hope she can't see mine. I think about all I've been through in the past four years and realize my mom has never deserted me. Boys left, friendships fell apart, but my mom was my solid rock. She never stopped loving me, even when she should have, and she never gave up on me. I know I'm not where I need to be in my life, but I tell myself that one day I will be.

I look at my dad, my eyes blurry. He holds me and tells me he'll see me at class on Monday. I try to laugh, but tears choke my throat. I don't know what I'll do without my daddy's protection. I try not to think about it.

In true Stanfill family tradition, we exchange envelopes—their letters to me, and my letter and CD to them. I made a CD of songs that remind me of our life together, eighteen years of memories packed into one tiny disc. "Home" by Michael Bublé is the first song. My mom will later tell me that when the song came on, they pulled over and held each other as they cried. I also included Michelle Branch's "Goodbye To You," a song from the CD my dad and I listened to on the way to father-daughter camp my freshman year of high school, when my great rebellion was just starting. Fleetwood Mac's "Landslide" is on there because when I was ten, my dad told me he was about to play the greatest song ever written; I took it literally and was sorely disappointed, but it still made it. "In My Daughter's Eyes" by Martina McBride is also on there. My mom and I deemed it our song when it first came out; she said it reminded her of how alive I was as a child.

♥

The day I left for college was one of those days when you put all your issues aside and love each other despite yesterday and the day before. I was hoping I'd be stronger on this day, that I wouldn't feel so connected to my parents, but you can't erase your childhood. More important, you can't shake unconditional love.

The next few days passed in a blur. I was more homesick than I thought I would be. Even so, I thrived, surrounded by so many new people. I loved making new friends. We quickly bonded with our suitemates when we all shared a bottle of wine, and we even met some girls from Atlanta down the hall. I was ecstatic to start sorority rush. Sororities are a big thing in the South, and where you got in seemed to determine your social status in college. My mom was in a sorority, my friends were all rushing, and I wanted affirmation that I fit in somewhere on this giant college campus. It never occurred to me that joining a sorority might be a life-changing event.

Rush On

We met our Pi Chi groups a few days before rush, and I found girls I loved. Our leader reminded me of a maternal friend I had back home. I was so excited to start over, a fresh start at a new school in a new sorority.

Day one was filled with parties, and by the end, I was so exhausted that I could barely stand. I'd made the same conversation at least ten times with a few five-minute breaks in between. I judged the sororities based on what most eighteen-year-old girls probably judge other girls on—clothes, chapter rooms, looks, and (lastly) personality. I picked a few sororities I liked, and my roommate and I went to bed around nine.

The next day was much the same but with one big change at the end—cuts were made that night. We all sat in a big line by last name; since I was in the *S* group, I was at the end. The girls in my group tried to talk, but we were so tired and nervous we ended up sitting in silence. I watched as some girls walked away all smiles and others filed out in tears, talking on their cell phones. I wasn't worried. I had my list of my top twelve between my sweaty palms, and I reviewed it every so often to make sure I still remembered.

Finally our group made it up to the computers. I sat in front of my computer screen and clicked on my name. I looked at the screen in shock. Only eight sororities had invited me back. Most of my friends had twelve or thirteen invite them back, so eight felt like a personal knock. *Eight out of sixteen—only half—want me* was all I kept thinking. Tears filled my eyes and threatened to spill over. I knew I had to accept all of the invitations; I didn't have a choice. I felt the too-familiar "the world is crashing down around me" feeling, and I tried to stay strong. More rejection. I didn't understand; what had I done to deserve this?

It was twelve o'clock in Atlanta, and after I left the computer, I called my mom in tears. "I only got invited back by eight," I sobbed into the phone.

I was inconsolable. This was a life-and-death situation. If I didn't get into a good sorority, I wouldn't go to the good parties and I wouldn't have the pretty friends. I tried to explain this to my mom, and she did her best to calm me down, but I was so hurt. Girls had met me and said that they couldn't see themselves being friends with me. I started to question everything I knew about myself. It was like being fourteen all over again, the pain of wanting so desperately to be a part of the popular crowd. I had built my life around fitting in, and now, my first week at a new college, I was already getting rejected. I thought I was good with people; maybe not. I thought I was pretty; maybe not. I thought I'd fit in on this campus; maybe not. My new friends did the best they could to console me, but they hadn't had the same situation; they weren't rejected by half of the sixteen sororities. Eventually, I consoled myself. There were still two sororities on my list that I liked, and I told myself as long as I could have those two on the last day, I'd be okay.

The next few days dragged on with a slow anticipation. I just wanted to get to the end. My emotions were fried, my heart was broken, and I was a nervous wreck. A couple of friends from my high school were going through rush with me, and we started comparing our favorites. They all loved Zeta, which a few of the older girls from our high school loved, and I was torn between Pi Phi and Zeta. I knew all my friends would be in Zeta and there'd be a lot of familiar faces, but this tiny voice kept whispering that I could start over, I could be different.

Somehow we reached the end, preference day, and I had two I liked, but in my head I'd already picked my favorite. I told myself that even if I didn't get it, I'd still end up in one I liked.

At the end of preference day, all one thousand girls in black dresses were herded like cattle down to the room where we'd list our preferences. I walked with one of my newfound friends, and we whispered about our favorites. She wanted Alpha Chi, and I was convinced I could find a place at Pi Phi.

I filled out my preference card in the order of my favorites, turned it in, and breathed a sigh of relief. I put it in the hands of the God I wasn't sure I believed in and figured His guess was as good as mine.

We had one final dinner with our rush group that had dwindled from sixteen girls to ten, and we laughed about the week. We all exchanged funny stories, and for a moment we were all friends, not yet divided by the Greek letters we wore.

My parents arrived early the next morning, and even though I'd seen them only a week before, it felt like much more time had passed. I felt like I'd gone through a lifetime of emotions in one week. They took me out to lunch, and I could barely eat, I was so nervous to get my bid. After lunch, we stood on the president's lawn and waited for the truck full of bids to come up the driveway. Girls were running around laughing, so happy to have all made it to this day. The truck pulled up honking, and we all got with our rush groups from the week. Our Pi Chi (group leader) made her way down the line, handing out our bids in alphabetical order. On the count of three we all opened them together in one big sorority-girl cheer. I'd gotten my first pick; I was a Pi Phi. I looked around for the other girls from home, and I watched as they all went running to the opposite side; they'd all gone Zeta.

I walked to the chapter room by myself and couldn't help but wonder if this was a mistake; I didn't know a single person in my new sorority. I told myself that this was what I had wanted, but now that it was right in front of me, I didn't know if it was. I wanted the familiarity of my old friends; I wanted to be back at home, not in a tiny dorm room. Instead, I was sitting in my new home surrounded by unfamiliar faces. This weird feeling wouldn't last long, though.

CHAPTER 9

A NEW SONG

MY FRESHMAN YEAR of college was a year of learning. I wanted to be different, but I didn't know how to get there. So college started the way high school ended: I attended parties with my sorority sisters and got drunk often. I enjoyed the freshman life. I made friends quickly. They were like me, but they had a Christian twist, and we formed a tight-knit group. Most of my new friends were religious, and they went to church on Sunday. They didn't smoke marijuana and rarely dropped the f-bomb. It was a lifestyle I wasn't used to.

After a few months of this, I met a new boy to call my own, but I hadn't totally left my old ways. Unfortunately, the first time I met his parents was when they caught us making out. They'd come to visit, and I was too drunk to go home, so I stayed at his house. It was embarrassing to say the least, but we kept dating. He came from a Christian home like I did but was one year older and was looking for a change from the way he'd been brought up. We'd spend hours talking about "spiritual things," and my mom screamed with joy when I told her we'd gone to church. I hadn't told her that I'd spent the night at his house before church. We didn't have sex, because we'd both been there and knew the emotional pain it caused, so we made the decision together to see if we could have a good relationship without sex.

To my shock, even though I wanted to have sex, I found we could have a deep emotional connection without it. I realized I didn't need sex to define a relationship. In fact, the relationship was much easier without sex. When we broke up, I cried for a few days, but the pain wasn't the same. We weren't connected physically like the relationships where I'd had sex, so I could move on without feeling like part of my heart had been ripped out.

It slowly became clear that it wasn't my family that had caused pain in my past; it was the decisions I'd been making. Here I was, 150 miles from my parents and finally free, and I still felt empty and alone. I still felt like my life was missing something. In a new place where no one knew my past, I was keenly aware that I could continue the life I'd had in high school or I could try something new. I remembered how unhappy and disgusted with myself I was in high school, so I opted for something different. Our sorority had a Bible study for the pledges, and I decided to go with one of my girlfriends who also had a Christian background. I remember telling my mom on the phone that I was joining my sorority's Bible study, and her response was perfect: "Oh my gosh, Tindell, tell me to sit down before you tell me stuff like that. I almost passed out."

You see, I wasn't planning on making *big* changes, just enough to round out the edges, clean up my reputation a little bit, and avoid reliving the heartache. My commitment was still halfhearted, and I spent the fall semester doing most of the same things but with a new emptiness. I'd go home from parties and be bored with the drinking. I completely stopped smoking and only drank socially. Gone were the days when I'd drink enough to pass out, and I realized you can get a lot done on Saturday and Sunday when you're not hungover. Meanwhile, my mom and I were building a real relationship. She actually liked the new guy I was dating and loved hearing about our weekly church attendance. My brothers were, as always, rooting for me. They'd call to check on me, to see how I was adjusting, and I was shocked when I realized how much I was beginning to depend on them. My dad and I had remained the closest through it all, and he encouraged me to move forward in life. Don't get me wrong—I hadn't made any huge changes yet; I was still partying and drinking with all my sorority sisters, but suddenly I realized my future was right in front of me and I had decisions to make. I knew that one day I wanted to be married, but the kind of guy I wanted to marry wouldn't marry the girl I was. I realized I wanted to be respected and trusted. I realized that I really wanted more in life.

My mom's timing was perfect when she told me that my brother was playing at a Christian conference in Nashville over Christmas break. Because I was open to change and searching, I decided to go. It was a big deal and an honor that he was playing, and I wanted to show him how proud I was of him. I wasn't expecting for it to change my life, but I did go in with an open mind, something I hadn't had in years. I went in knowing I was unhappy and wondering if there was something better. In other words, I gave God a tiny space to move in, and He blew it apart.

While I was there, I heard Beth Moore talk about the pit of sin and how God could lift us out of it, and I knew she was talking to me. When my brother came onstage and sang "Jesus Paid It All," I fell to my knees and prayed He would wash my stains away. It was a glorious moment. I felt relief for the first time in years, and I knew change had to happen in my life. There was no doubt it would be hard, but I didn't care. I wanted healing. I wanted relief from the gut-wrenching pain I was bringing on myself. I wanted God to place my feet on solid ground. I begged for forgiveness for my long list of sins, and I was washed clean as my brother sang a new song over my life, the same song I so desperately wanted to believe all those years ago. "Jesus paid it all; all to him I owe. . . ."

That day, my own sound track started anew. God replaced the depressing, painful tracks with songs of grace, and I smiled genuinely for the first time in what felt like years.

God didn't care about my yesterdays. In that moment, He washed away all my pain, and I became a new person. At the end of the service I ran up to my parents, and in one tearful apology, we put our family back together. I called Kristian and his wife, and they met me at a coffee shop. I told them God had changed me, and I was sorry for all the hurt. They hugged me and told me it was all forgotten. I'd spent years trying to destroy family bonds that I realized now could never be broken.

I wish I could say that I walked away and my life changed just like that! But just because you love God doesn't mean all your sinful desires will fade away. I had to unlearn the things I'd taught myself for the past four years. I had to be obedient when I didn't feel like it, and I had to learn that what my heart wanted wasn't always what was best.

I still had the same needs, but now I had to find something lasting with which to fulfill them. Sleeping around seemed like a bad idea; drinking until I passed out didn't look all that appealing; and my friendships felt very surface level. I knew I had to make changes, but I was lost in this new life. Most of my friends were still living the same life as before, but I knew I couldn't. I'd reconnected with my family, but they were a hundred miles away.

So I did the only thing I knew to do at the time. I prayed. I prayed God would use me to help girls who had a similar story to mine. I prayed God would send me friends to help me, and I prayed He would lead me. I got more involved in a Bible study and started attending a campus ministry, small steps back to real life. I took a leadership position in my sorority where I was in charge of "standards," which basically meant I was everyone's mom. Since I was one of the few girls who didn't drink, I was appointed to mother all the girls who did. If the girls didn't follow the rules, I was the one enforcing the punishment. In a sorority of two hundred girls known for its parties, I had my work cut out for me. Every time I walked into a party, beer bottles were lowered, and girls untangled themselves from whichever fraternity boys they'd found. My mom would laugh when I complained that the girls just couldn't behave. She shook her head and said, "Oh, how the times have changed." I had to laugh sometimes too; God really does have a sense of humor. He decided to place me in charge of the rules when months earlier I was hell bent on breaking them.

The hardest part about coming back to Christ was

learning that He wanted me to have a relationship with Him, not just follow a set of rules. The only thing I knew about following Christ was that there was a set of rules Christians were supposed to follow. The rules were not what I needed, though. I needed to change my lifestyle, but I needed a *reason* to change my lifestyle. I needed a better story to be written in my life, and I wasn't going to do this on my own. But since I was kind of immature in this stage of my return to faith, I became obsessed with rules. Even though all my old friends knew my past and liked me better when I wasn't a Christian, I kept going forward. When I stopped drinking, I lost most of my friends, and the only thing to comfort me at night were the rules I clung to so tightly.

I did my best to show mercy and grace, but because I had a hard time separating the relationship aspect of Christianity from the rules, I was more of a dictator than an ambassador of grace. I should have been more understanding about what my sorority sisters were going through; I'd gone through the same thing months earlier. I could have proven my point without being a tyrant, but I didn't know how to do that. See, God didn't care about the rules. What He really cared about was that I loved those girls. All I really needed to do was live a different life from the crowd, but that was beyond radical for me. I didn't know how to distinguish being different from being a dictator. (I think that's something a lot of Christians struggle with!) And because I was so new to this side of authority, I didn't understand that God cares more about love than anything else. The rules are in place to help us, but they're not what He's about. I had a great opportunity to show my sorority sisters what was really important in life. I had a chance to show them how much God loves them, but instead I drank in my power and tightened the rules.

God has never won people over with dos and don'ts; He wins them over with His compassion and love. And then, after He wins their hearts, He guides them to a more fulfilling life. The rules are nothing; the relationship is everything.

When I took baby steps toward God, I learned I didn't want to live the life I had been living. I wanted to be different. It was like a light clicked on in the darkness, and I could finally see what I had really been doing to myself. I could see I wasn't happy. Since I'd lost most of my old friends for my new life, I was lonely and begging God for new friendships. As always, He listened and came through.

Heather was my youngest brother's best friend; she was also the girl he loved. They bonded over a spring break mission trip, and since she was two years older than he, they were waiting to date. I'd met her a few times, but because I was so self-involved, we never really connected. Then she decided to attend Auburn, and she showed up around the time I was making huge lifestyle changes. We bonded during one long car ride back to college and became fast friends. She was everything I'd prayed for, and I learned more from her than I ever thought I could. She helped me navigate the Bible, and I kept her entertained with stories from my crazy past. I taught her to give grace, and she taught me to be a godly woman.

After I decided not to live with my sorority sisters anymore, Heather and I decided to live together with another close friend, and we had more fun than I ever thought possible. Heather introduced me to other awesome Christian girls, and some of my best college memories are the ones we shared in our tiny apartment during my junior year. The three of us would sit around with a tub of ice cream until four in the morning, laughing and telling stories. Heather helped me navigate my new faith and even a few heartaches. She was there when I met my husband, and when I got married, she stood by my side as my maid of honor. One of the great things about our friendship was that she was best friends with my youngest brother, which gave me a chance to bond with him. He'd come visit and go to football games with us, and before I knew it, I had another great friend—my brother. I'm proud to say that I gave the final shove that pushed them to date, and last fall she became my sister.

It's stories like these that show how great God is. I could never have orchestrated those events on my own, but God could. He knew when I'd need Heather, and He knew she'd be a part of my life forever. God does what no one else can do; He works things out according to His plan to prosper our future (see Jeremiah 29:11). I could have fumbled my way through college and come out slightly bruised, but instead I let Him lead, and I came out with a loving husband, great friends, and a family I would do anything for. God did that, not me.

Christmas 2006 was a great one. It was my first Christmas home since I'd committed my life to Christ; my life was just beginning to show the changes I was making, and I'd asked for a Bible. Lo and behold, there was a tiny red Bible sticking out of my stocking when I came down on Christmas morning. I skimmed through it and read the Christmas story while our whole family gathered around the fire in our living room. We had the first peaceful Christmas in years. Our family has a tradition on all major holidays: we go around and say what we're thankful for. When my turn came, my eyes filled with tears, and I told my family that I was thankful for their unconditional love. My dad was the first one to stand, and he wrapped me in a huge hug and whispered, "You were easy to love."

God. It always comes back to Him. Every time someone wonders how I made it through: God. Every time a parent asks me what saved my life: God. Every time someone wants to know how I never got arrested or physically hurt: God. It was always God, like the ending of a great love story where you find out that the guy who was always there was "the one" all along. It was always Him. He never left. He let me take the reins, but He never left: God. In the midst of my decisions—and even some of the harsh consequences—God never left.

God is a great storyteller; He knows how to include all the elements: suspense, comedy, love, glory, and sometimes tragedy. It all points back to Him—at least all the good parts do. I'd like to think God doesn't use tragedy, that He only uses the good things in life for His glory, but my life is proof that this just isn't true.

My closest girlfriend in high school was my partner in crime. If I was drunk, so was she. We smoked together, drank together, and battled life together. We were there for each other in the good and bad. Her mom's cancer, after a remission, returned when we were in high school, and since we didn't know how to handle pain, we drank. When we parted ways, I cleaned up and she became addicted. Then her mom passed away, and she hit rock bottom. Her close friends tried to help, but she ended up in rehab. Today she's one of the strongest, most beautiful people I know. She's a huge inspiration to me because she's felt death's sting and lived to tell about it. I've had it easy in comparison to her, but God has used the tragedy in her life to speak to others.

God uses tragedy in all our lives. He is always working a story in your life. Each part has been carefully constructed—preparing you, growing you, changing you, molding you—to better His Kingdom. Sometimes it takes pain, but the pain always turns into something greater. He isn't just working through your story, He's working through everyone else's, even the unlikeliest. People love to think they can run from God, but where can you hide from the God of the universe? You may think you can hide your heart, but even if you bury yourself in evil schemes, He uses them to His advantage. God knew I would come back to His Kingdom and that I would write this book. He knew I was going to further His glory from my ashes, because He is that kind of God.

God is not too good for irony and symbolism. In the Bible, He plays off them, demonstrating a deep connection with His people's hearts through each generation. God asked Abraham to sacrifice his son Isaac (see Genesis 22:1-14), giving us a human picture of His own heart-wrenching sacrifice. David became king at age thirty (see 2 Samuel 5:4), the same age that Jesus was when He started His earthly ministry. Jesus was a storyteller, a master of His language, seeing that even the small things would captivate the people He created. He displayed His deep-seated devotion to us by striving to relate to us in a human way. He came to earth as a man and died as a man to cover all our sins. He lived like us, lived among us, and taught us. He did all that so that He could have a relationship with us—with you. Sin was separating us from God, but Jesus bridged the gap. Because He died, taking all our sins on Himself, and He rose again, overcoming death, we can start over every single day. I can have a full relationship with my Creator, and if God can forgive me, I can forgive myself.

In His holiness, God chose to become human. It was His way of courting us, making us feel that we can truly relate to the God of the universe. By suffering as humans suffer, feeling as humans feel, and accepting the possibility of rejection, God humbled Himself when He was something so much greater, simply so we could understand. He sits on a glorious throne *and* at our doorstep. He is praised by all creation, yet He is rejected by mere humans. He knew our minds could never grasp all that He is, so He came up with a way to relate to us. He tells life's greatest lessons in the form of children's stories. He does miracles to grab our attention, and thousands of years later we're still amazed at His irony, sense of humor, and powerful love. Our God is not a boring God, nor does He act in vain. He makes purposeful moves to demonstrate His deep connection to our souls. He makes us laugh in grief, smile in pain, trust what we cannot see. We often want to rattle off reasons for things that seem too coincidental, but what if we started giving credit where credit is due?

I Say the F-Word at Church Camp

One of the many times I got caught having a party at my house, my parents were looking for a unique way to punish me. Grounding me for months on end wasn't working, and to be honest, they were tired of me being around the house. They decided to give church camp a go. My brother Kristian was leading worship at the camp, so they figured, *What's the worst that could happen?* They really underestimated me.

The camp was in Panama City, Florida, and I conned one of my best friends into going with me. We were placed with some other girls who were labeled "wild," and I quickly made friends with all of them. We'd skip the sessions and get in constant arguments with our small-group leader on why we had to wear one-piece bathing suits instead of our bikinis. Whenever the small-group leader tried to get me to answer questions, I'd spout off some smart answer about why I didn't need God. During the worship sessions, they had security guards around the hotel so none of the kids could leave the sessions. Once, one of my youth pastors found me yelling at a security guard about why I should be allowed to go up to my room. I finally ran past him and dropped the f-bomb. The small-group leaders and youth pastors at camp were left shaking their heads and praying the worship leader's little sister would straighten up.

Four years later, I became an intern at the same camp. One afternoon I was setting up for the youth leader meeting when I heard a voice I barely recognized calling my name. I turned around to find my small-group leader from several years ago standing at the door, mouth open.

"What are you doing here?" was all she could manage.

"I'm an intern," I said with a smile.

She just started laughing; there wasn't much else to do. We were both amazed at the way God had brought me back to the camp I'd fought so hard to leave years earlier. As an intern, I dedicated a summer of sweat and tears to that camp and the young people in it. The best part was at the start of every week when I got to share my stories of being a rebellious camper who refused to wear a one-piece swimsuit.

God really does have a sense of humor. I think this was His way of showing me how He was in control even when I was out of control. He knew that one day I wouldn't be fighting the security guard, I would *be* the security guard. He knew that one day I'd be working for Him instead of against Him, and He revealed His grand sense of humor when He asked me to go back to the camp to show everyone what miraculous things He can do. I promise that if you knew me during my teen years, you'd agree it was a miraculous change.

CHAPTER 10

BABY STEPS TO FOUR O'CLOCK

FEEL FREE TO slow clap at this point. The battle is won. I've come over to the other side, and if this were a movie, the closing scene would be a tearful redemption followed by the credits. But becoming a Christian is just the start. If it were the climax, then everything else would be a piece of cake. When I became a Christian, my life felt like it really started. If my life looked like those plot charts teachers draw in ninth-grade English, we'd just be starting to climb the hill. Redemption and grace are amazing, but they're just part of who God is. God is made of blessings and plans. Once I was redeemed, He started His story in my life. I was no longer writing alone; I had the best

Narrator in the world alongside me, pushing me down the right path.

Becoming a Christian doesn't mean all your problems fade away, and it definitely doesn't mean all your old habits die with your old self. You'll still be tempted to act the same, tempted to put your hope in the same things, and tempted to think the same. The hardest part of Christianity isn't accepting Christ; it's what comes after that. It's when He asks you to walk away from relationships, friends, and a life you were accustomed to. God asks you to make these decisions so you can see that He only wants what is best for your life. If you can walk away from the really hard stuff, then huge blessings are waiting at the other end.

God asked me to give up a lot; I had formed a life around my addictions, and walking away meant being alone. I had never really clicked with church girls. I hated being alone. I loved being surrounded by a group of people, but He was asking me to be alone for a while. When I finally walked away from my old life, He was waiting with a life full of blessings.

Once I removed myself from the group of girls I'd always partied with, I became really close with my family, which provided me with Christian relationships and a way to explore church. I started going home for family functions and talking to my family more on the phone while I was away. I found out that I really loved talking to my mom. I realized that while I'd given up a lot of old friends, I'd gained relationships that were there the whole time. I looked forward to the rare times we all got together. And being with my entire family was my new high. They were so loving and wise, and I knew I didn't deserve their love.

It seemed that after I showed Him that I would truly give up anything for Him, God gave me the desires of my heart. He asked me to be obedient and take small steps toward Him. He didn't ask that I change everything in a day; maybe He would have liked that, but life isn't that easy. I just had to take baby steps toward Him; and the closer I got, the more I realized I didn't want to smoke, or drink, or fall back into my bad dating habits. I realized the more I got to know Jesus, the more I really loved Him. The more I loved Him, the more I wanted to be sold out to Him and Him alone.

God is cool like that. Once you really dig in deep to who He is, you won't be able to get enough. I had dry seasons and times when I questioned where I was going, but once I let Him fill my heart, my heart could never give Him up. I knew I couldn't go back to my old life now that I had the alternative.

That was the main difference between when I followed Christ at fourteen and when I recommitted my life to Him at age nineteen. I actually got to know Him. I learned everything about Jesus that I always claimed to understand. I learned the true meaning of forgiveness and grace, and when I learned them, I put them into practice. I learned what it looked like to be selfless, and I started putting others first. I was shocked that I found tremendous joy in simply doing the things that God commanded of me. I learned that He had put the "rules" in place not to punish me but to protect me.

I think there's a tendency in Christianity to learn the answers and not the God, to learn what to say so you sound like you get it. Then, if you just live within the obvious boundaries, you'll be okay. I tried this for a while and I was unimpressed; my old life looked like more fun. I didn't want to watch movies alone every Friday night or grow to be an old maid with a houseful of cats. But over time, the more I actually got to know Jesus, the more I realized He didn't want that for me either. I got to know who He was on earth, who He wanted to be in my life, and why He wanted certain things for me. I understood the relationship went way beyond a set of rules.

Jesus Who?

Jesus isn't a trend. God is like a classic style, not a trendy knockoff. That's not always appealing, but it's what's great about God: He never changes. He's committed to you. His love is unwavering, unchanging, and absolute. Having this knowledge is cooler than any Apple product.

In a world where cravings come and go and trends fade

daily with the sun, God remains constant. He doesn't need to dress truth up in the latest jeans and Converse shoes. He can wear those same ancient robes and remain the most influential man in the world. What a comfort when fitting in never seems possible or comes at the cost of pieces of your soul. Think about it: as soon as we get a handle on this season's fashions, they change. As soon as we figure out what the group expects of us, it all shifts beneath our feet, and once again we struggle to keep up. God doesn't change. Through each era, He watches as Satan dresses sin up in different outfits and people fumble to make themselves happy, while He is always there. From free love to freeloader, sin is the same. It takes different forms and promises different things, but that's always to disguise the truth that God is the only thing that satisfies. Sin is deceit, and God is truth; you can't have both. Perhaps this is why hypocrisy makes us so angry—because we know that sin and godliness do not go together. You cannot fully embrace who God is and continue to live in sin.

First John 3:9 puts it this way: "No one who is born of God will continue to sin, because God's seed remains in him; he cannot go on sinning, because he has been born of God."

In my life, sin sidled in through my love of popularity and boys. I'm not saying that either of these things when handled correctly is bad, but when they define you, there's a problem. My climb to the top of the popularity food chain cost me almost everything, and my fall from those heights left me clinging to alcohol and drugs in hopes of numbing the pain. My desire to be loved left me with a desperately broken heart at the age of eighteen. And yet, at the end of it all, God was waiting.

Christians as a whole like to talk a big game, but when it comes down to the decisions we make daily, we can be pretty hypocritical. We love to talk about grace, but we don't always give it. We love to tell others to forgive, but we can hold grudges for a lifetime. We love to quote things about loving your neighbor, but then we talk behind others' backs. Prayer time can become a gossip reel, and being mean to others is too often justified by labeling them "sinners." I believe this is one of the main reasons people are turned off by Christianity.

Let me take a moment to say that no matter how hypo-critical your neighborhood Christian is, no matter how hypocritical the youth group leader might be, no matter how many times you've seen a righteous, megapublic Christian leader or politician turn out to be the opposite of what he said he was, Jesus didn't live this way. Jesus taught us to love others, and then He ate dinner at the house of the most hated (see Matthew 9:10). Jesus told us to practice grace, and then He forgave Peter for denying Him three times. Jesus was never a hypocrite, and a life with Christ is 100 percent about living for Jesus, not about what your fellow church members think.

If this is what's holding you back from Christianity, then I challenge you to forget the other "Christians" you know and get to know Jesus. You'll find that He always sticks to what He says and never judges unfairly. You're always welcome at His throne, and He prefers if you come with your sin in hand. He doesn't demand that you clean up first, just that you have an open heart. Living a life of hypocrisy is living a life of sin, and if you observe hypocritical Christians and think that's how Jesus lived, trust me—you haven't really gotten to know Him.

So what does choosing to trust in Christ mean for high school teens? It means you might not be part of the "popular" crowd, unless you can somehow manage to be like my brother Taylor, who was totally cool and pulled off drinking O'Doul's (nonalcoholic beer) while the rest of his high school class got wasted on Bud Light. It means your way may not be easy, but God says in the Bible that this world will not understand us and will challenge our way of life. Truly following Christ is countercultural, and it will make people wonder. Some of those people may even call themselves Christians as they judge, condemn, or ignore you, but you will find there is much, much more to grace than that.

Matthew 10:22 says, "All men will hate you because of me, but he who stands firm to the end will be saved." John 15:18-20 makes it even clearer:

If the world hates you, keep in mind that it hated me first. *If you belonged to the world, it would love you as its own.* As it is, you do not belong to the world, but I have chosen you out of the world. That is why the world hates you. Remember the words I spoke to you: "No servant is greater than his master." If they persecuted me, they will persecute you also. If they obeyed my teaching, they will obey yours also. (emphasis added)

This makes sense if you break it apart. Satan is the king of darkness; Jesus is the Light of the World. Satan despises God, so people who are deceived by Satan come to believe they don't need God. Satan hates truth, and he convinces his followers that truth is boring and plain and offers nothing. Satan wants you to believe that what God is offering you is social suicide and you'll never be happy. He wants you to believe you can't make it without the things of this world. I believed that; I thought I needed the alcohol and the drugs, but in reality I needed a Savior. John 1:10-13 says,

[Jesus] was in the world, and though the world was made through him, the world did not recognize him. He came to that which was his own, but his own did not receive him. Yet to all who received him, to those who believed in his name, he gave the right to become children of God—children born not of natural descent, nor of human decision or a husband's will, but born of God.

God makes it very clear here that people who believe that the world has more to offer than He does have swallowed a lie—so much so that they don't recognize their own Father. You might think you can see and that you have a handle on the darkness, but you don't even know where the light is. How can you know where you stand when no one around you has a lamp? I didn't believe I was hurting myself; I didn't believe I was doing anything wrong; and worst of all, I didn't believe I needed a Savior. Then the lamp was raised in my life and I saw all the demons lurking around me, demons I had created. My heart had been ripped to shreds, and my body was covered in scars. Until I found the light, I couldn't see any of this, because I was standing in the darkness.

I know we don't like to think of God as hating anything, but God hates sin because He loves us so much. He hates the distractions of this world that cause us to forget about our real purpose. He loved us so much He gave His *only Son* to us; it makes sense that He would be angered when we reject His precious gift for things that mean nothing. The real reason we're here has nothing to do with what we can gain, but rather what we can give.

God weeps when His children end up self-destructing because Satan has convinced them that there's no other way. Though God weeps for your pain, He knows a way out, a way that will forever glorify Him.

Satan wants you to self-destruct. I could dress that up in pretty church words with less intimidating meanings, but until we grasp the truth, we will never recognize the lies. God wants only good for you, a great abundant life full of joy, both now and in the life to come. Satan wants you chained to this world by the bondage of your sin. If you think I'm extreme, then he has you fooled. If you think you're dabbling in something you can handle, then you've already put on the handcuffs. I dabbled once. I drank my first beer at fifteen, and in three years' time I was addicted to alcohol and drugs and had lost my virginity. I was living with devout Christian parents and brothers, but it has nothing to do with family. Heaven isn't a club; you don't get in because of who you know.

It wasn't for lack of guidance that I made these mistakes. It was because my eyes were covered by the lies I bought into. I went to church. I knew the stories. But knowing has nothing to do with believing. I dabbled and then drowned. Sin is one small step after another that take you leaps and bounds away from God.

Some coyote hunters have a way of killing their prey: they make a blood Popsicle with a razor blade in the middle. The coyote comes to the smell of the blood, begins to lick it, and keeps licking it, drinking in the taste of an animal's blood. Then he gets to the razor blade, licks it, and begins to cut himself. However, the coyote can't distinguish between his own blood and the other blood. So he keeps licking, drinking his own blood and slowly dying. Each lick is fatal, but each lick tastes so good. The hunter, meanwhile, is waiting in the bushes for the prey to die.

Sin is much the same. The first few licks might be harmless, but at some point you'll get to the razor blade. At some point you're going to start killing yourself one decision at a time. One beer won't hurt me, *lick*. Two beers are no big deal, *lick*. I can fool around with this guy, *lick*. Maybe if we just took it a little further . . . I mean, I really love him, *lick*. One puff won't kill me, *lick*. Before you know it you have drained yourself of your own blood while Satan sits behind the bushes and smiles his big *GQ* grin. Then there is God weeping at your side, watching the beautiful thing He created killing itself.

When you were slaves to sin, you were free from the control of righteousness. What benefit did you reap at that time from the things you are now ashamed of? Those things *result in death*! But now that you have been *set free from sin* and have become slaves to God, the benefit you reap leads to holiness, and the result is eternal life. For the

wages of sin is death, but the gift of God is eternal
life in Christ Jesus our Lord.

ROMANS 6:20-23 (EMPHASIS ADDED)

So here you are, uncool and fighting something that
wants to kill you. Sounds more like a good novel than
your life. But it is your life; you're fighting a crucial battle
for your soul. God has equipped you with everything you
need to fight the enemy, and He has already won, but that
doesn't mean the battle's over. God's given you a game
plan; you just have to heed His guidance. Until we live
in a sinless place, we will have to fight the ruler of this
crumbling world.

Here's my take on a pretty well-known passage about
how God equips us:

> Put on the full armor of God, so that you can take
> a stand against the devil's schemes. For our fight
> is not against our flesh and blood, but against the
> dark forces that have taken control of this world,
> the evil spiritual forces. Put on the full armor of
> God, so that you can make your stand when the
> world comes out to get you. Stand firm with the
> belt of truth (know truth so that you can outsmart
> lies; we cannot rebuke lies if we do not know
> truth), the breastplate of righteousness (keep
> your body righteous so when the devil tempts

you with fleshly desire you answer with God's
righteousness rather than weakness), and with
your feet firmly planted in readiness (never believe
you are immune to the struggles of this world,
otherwise it will be easy to catch you off guard).
In addition to all this, take up your shield of faith
(unwavering trust in the Lord's promises); with
this you can block all the arrows of the evil one.

EPHESIANS 6:11-16 (PARAPHRASED)

CHAPTER 11

WHAT DOES DIFFERENT LOOK LIKE?

ONE MORE PERIOD TO GO. I tell myself that every time I have to remind the kids there's no talking during a test. I'm lucky they had a test today, because I'm not in the mood to raise my voice. I hate raising my voice. Silence has become a big part of my life. It helps me think, and with middle schoolers, I have a lot to think about.

The oddball in the class asked me to call her Inker, and the other kids snickered. I could tell she marches to the beat of her own drum when she asked if she could read me an excerpt from her dragon book. I can only assume her new name is a character from her sci-fi/fantasy novel. She was the first to finish her test; she's probably off-the-charts smart. Her tie-dyed dragon T-shirt hangs over faded jeans, and when she looks at me it's as if she doesn't see me.

There's one in every class—the kid the other kids laugh at, the oddball or the social misfit. They've perfected the art of not seeming to care. True or not, it's almost as if they don't notice. Sometimes I get the feeling the only reason the other kids make fun of them is because they're jealous that the misfits have so clearly staked out their own identities, or think they have. By rejecting the whole concept of "fitting in," misfits each get to be their own person. I wonder who it's harder to be: the misfit who has her own identity or the girl who's just another face in the crowd.

You have to lose so much to be part of the "in" crowd. You have to give up your identity, your values, and anything else that's deemed uncool. But to be different, really different from the crowd, you need nothing more than yourself. You can be free from other people's expectations of you, knowing that after the teenage years fade away you'll be left with something solid: your true self. I bet the misfits have learned early how much family means (maybe by having one, maybe by not having one) and the value of one good friend. I have a feeling Inker understands more of herself at fourteen than most kids her age.

I wish I'd had the courage to stand apart from the crowd. I wish I'd had the courage to chance loneliness to keep my values. Why is it that the fear of the unknown will keep us from almost anything? I thought being uncool would kill me, but a few years down the road, I realize being cool doesn't really matter. The crowd I was dying to get into has long since faded, and in its place are the relationships I tried the hardest to leave behind. If only I'd had the courage to be different. I might not have as many good stories, but I'd have a lot fewer scars.

After class, I let Inker read me an excerpt from her book. She put on her best Shakespearean accent and read me a few paragraphs. I have no idea what she said, but I told her she was an excellent reader. She smiled proudly; she already knew. She told me she read at a twelfth-grade level at the age of fourteen. If nothing more, she was honest. What I wouldn't give to have that kind of confidence in myself even today. I came home from work that night, tired and not feeling like myself, and lost myself in a few good shows. For a moment, I wanted to be Inker.

My dad once told me that normal is just a setting on the washing machine, and the longer I live, the more I see that to be true. Take heart in the fact that there is no such thing as normal. If there were, we'd live in a very boring place. You may find people who enjoy the same things as you, dress like you, or even look like you, but I guarantee that even if you're in the majority where you are now, you're in the minority somewhere else. I grew up in an area where everyone was like me: white, middle class, comfortable families. After college, I moved to Houston with my husband and quickly realized I was the minority in my new city.

God needs many different types of people to fulfill His purpose of spreading the gospel. You may have flipped to the back cover of this book, looked at my picture, and immediately thought, *What's* she *going to tell me about God?* Or maybe you and I look similar, and that's why you bought this book in the first place—you could relate to me. As universal as I might attempt to be, I'll not be able to minister as well to some as I can to others. You are perfect for whatever God wants to accomplish through you. Having the strength to be different is one of the hardest things you might ever do, but is it harder than living with decisions you will forever regret? No! Is it harder than telling your fiancé that you just couldn't wait for him? No! Being different is hard, but so is living with regrets or consequences of decisions you made to be a part of the crowd.

Take a minute to breathe and tell yourself that high school is not forever. If you don't belong now, it's not the end of the world—rather, it's just a tiny glimpse of the world. Think about this: research has shown that kids from ages fifteen through the early twenties have a hard time grasping the idea of the future because their brains aren't fully developed. In other words, you really can't grasp all the future can hold. Today might feel like the rest of your life, but let me assure you, it's not!

Different doesn't mean you have to wear those corny Christian T-shirts that change popular sayings into Christian ones. It doesn't mean you have to stay home on

Friday night and read the Bible. And it doesn't mean you can't enjoy TV shows, popular music, or alcohol when you're twenty-one if it fits your beliefs. It means you live a different type of life. You stand out because God resides in you, not because you wear a T-shirt that says, "Jesus died for MY SPACE in heaven" (sorry in advance if you own that shirt).

Once I became a Christian, I knew I had to start living a different life, and for me different was terrifying. I'd built my life around not sticking out, around blending with the in crowd, and now I was forced to abandon my faith or stand alone.

I was in a sorority that mainly consisted of either party girls or Sunday-only Christians. I was very different from most of the girls when I gave up drinking, and even though I loved them dearly, I knew I couldn't live like they were. I didn't quit talking to them, but I started staying sober when we went out. I made changes that showed something had happened on the inside that made me different from how I'd been. Was it easy? *No.* I hated it. I watched as the other girls had what seemed like a wonderful time, and I was left driving. I had to slowly learn how to have fun without the parties and alcohol. I made small steps away from that lifestyle, and God remained faithful and brought me great Christian friends.

I went on to have a wonderful college experience, meet the man of my dreams, and get married right out of college. I was more fulfilled than I ever thought I could be. I realized after "giving up" my party lifestyle that I wasn't actually giving anything up. God's Word (truth) is a "lamp to my feet" (Psalm 119:105), and it's only when you have a light that you notice you've been living in the dark. Many times God does not reveal this to you until you've been obedient and given up what you clung to so tightly.

To be honest, I had a hard time letting go of two things in particular: boys and alcohol. Typically, when there are boy problems, it's because you have "daddy issues." But I don't have that excuse. I have a great father. I'm a psychologist's nightmare (I know because from ages sixteen to eighteen I puzzled many of them). I just have boy issues. I craved attention from boys, as many teenage girls do, and to me my beauty was my only asset. Alcohol gave me the confidence I needed to be who boys wanted me to be. When I first became a Christian, I was so in love with the Lord, but I was having a hard time giving up my bad dating habits and alcohol. I tried every way possible to justify drinking, and in the moment I could always manage to convince myself that if I drank a little but didn't get drunk, then I'd be okay. I knew God was pleading with me to stop; He knew I was hurting my body and making decisions that left me filled with guilt. But I was still dabbling, still putting my foot in the waters of sin while I clung tightly to my Bible.

The summer after my freshman year of college I was really battling what I wanted and what I knew God was calling me to do. I have to reiterate that just because you become a Christian, it doesn't mean that what you want and what God wants for you are instantly one and the same. I didn't have a lot of Christian friends, so I went out with my friends from high school to the college near my hometown. While I was there, I ran into an ex of mine who I dated for a minute after I lost my first love, and I immediately fell into my habit of neediness. I wanted so desperately to be loved. I still didn't understand that sex does not mean love. I began to drink, just a few shots to kill the pain of longing, but it just got stronger. I was drowning out God's voice telling me I didn't have to do this, that He loved me deeply. I didn't care; I wanted to be loved that night.

To this day, the details of that night are a blur to me. I didn't end up with my ex. Somehow, I ended up with a stranger. I woke up in a strange bed with the taste of throw-up fresh on my tongue. I wasn't dressed, and there was a condom wrapper on the floor. I guessed what had happened. . . .

Plan B

We drove past the building in downtown Atlanta three times before we actually found it. A homeless man sat at the corner with a shopping cart full of his belongings and watched my best friend's BMW X5 drive back and forth. We finally parked behind the brown, nondescript building and found the elevator. The sign beside each floor showed us where we were going: Level 5—Planned Parenthood. A man in a business suit inside another office watched as I pressed the button. I knew he was judging me, and I couldn't blame him. I wished I could explain, wished I could tell him I was a good girl. I wished so much that I wasn't at this place making my way to somewhere I never wanted to be.

When we made it to the waiting room, I signed in and took the appropriate forms, and we sat down. My best friend tried to make me smile, but I was too ashamed. As I looked around, hopelessness seemed to cover the room like a dark cloud. Most of the women were older, a few joined by their boyfriends or husbands. A few had children on their hip; one little boy was crying. It smelled like a doctor's office, but not a very clean one. I tried to focus on the forms—just information about my sexual activity. There was a place to mark if you'd been raped. I wondered if I could put a question mark there. The truth was, I didn't know. Maybe I'd consented, but maybe I hadn't. That wasn't why I was here, though; I hadn't come for counseling. I'd come for the Plan B pill. I had come because I wanted to make absolutely sure that my one mistake didn't lead to a lifetime of regret—even if it meant doing something I didn't believe in.

I turned in my forms and waited for the lady at the counter to call my name, a large, stern woman who gave me a look that felt so cold. I thought I knew what she was thinking: *Why is this rich white girl in downtown Atlanta for the Plan B pill?* I wished I could tell her my story, but I couldn't. I wasn't entirely sure how I'd ended up there myself.

I was feeling so much emotional pain at that moment that I wanted to scream. Every look felt like a judgmental stare; every roll of the eyes felt like it was pointed in my direction. I was terrified and angry at so many people. I was mad at myself for getting into this situation. I was mad at the guy for not knowing when a girl was too drunk. I was scared and shaken because maybe he did know when a girl was too drunk and had me anyway.

Mostly I was devastated that I'd let this happen. I was ashamed and confused at the choice I'd made when I was supposed to be walking the path of righteousness. I was supposed to be a Christian, but here I was sitting in Planned Parenthood, asking for a pill I didn't even know if I agreed with. Before this moment, I'd claimed that the Plan B pill was abortion. Now that I was here, it felt like my saving grace.

When they finally called me back, I looked at my friend, and she gave me a reassuring smile. I'd have to do this part alone. I walked into a small room with another woman and sat in front of her desk. She didn't even look up from my papers; she just asked what I was here for. I lied. I told her I'd had unprotected sex with my boyfriend. More guilt. I figured at this point lying was the least of my worries. She still didn't look up.

"So you want the Plan B pill?"

"Yes," was the only response I could muster.

"That will be forty dollars," she said, and rattled off instructions I didn't catch. I handed her the money, and she handed me a brown sack. I didn't even check to see if it was the right pill. Instead, I shuffled out of the room with tears threatening to soak my face.

Finally safe with my friend, we headed for the car to go home. As we left, I wondered how many times the other girls and women in the waiting room had gone through what I'd gone through, or worse. I wanted to tell myself it wasn't a big deal—that everyone makes mistakes—but I knew it was a lie. I felt so much shame I could barely think on the way home. I'd promised myself I was going to be different, but here I was making mountains of mistakes again. My heart ached. I was so lost in the pain of shame I didn't even want to ask for the Lord's forgiveness. I didn't know what to confess. Looking out the window, I played the night's events back in my head once more: a few shots here, then a drink at the bar, then nothing. Just blankness where there should be memories.

The Aftermath

I made a decision that day to never get drunk again. I promised God I wouldn't touch alcohol until I was twenty-one, and then I would only handle it responsibly. God had asked me to obey His laws, but I thought He was trying to keep me from fun. The truth was that He was trying to keep me from deep pain.

Like the coyote hunter, Satan had me believe that I would stop before I hit the razor blade, but I just kept licking. Hear me when I write that God can wash away any sin, but He does not wash away your memory. I'm forever left with the memories of my past, and there are some days when those memories are so real and so shameful and so painful that all I can do is fall on my knees and pray that God gives me relief. This is what sin looks like—decisions that will change your life.

I wish that summer night after my freshman year of college had been different, but even though it was unlike anything I'd done before, for my friends it wasn't that unusual. Some of them had experienced being taken advantage of or giving their bodies when their minds were unwilling. The call to be different is hard and takes a lot of strength, but it doesn't prompt years of regret from mistakes or traumas like these. It doesn't bring the shame and brokenness of going to rehab or the heartache of losing a friend to an addiction. I'm not downplaying loneliness, rejection, or hurt. I'm saying that though loneliness brings pain, it does not haunt you like regret does. I'm saying that though rejection can cause deep heartache, it doesn't tear your soul apart like sexual promiscuity. God is asking you to be different not because He wants you to suffer but because the alternative is something you don't want to experience.

I know what you're thinking: *If drinking is so bad, why does it look so fun?* Well, here's the truth: it looks fun because sometimes it is. Let me tell you what it's not, though: it's not fulfilling, it's not satisfying, it doesn't make you a better person, it doesn't foster friendships that last, it's not selfless, it's not lasting, and it's not going to make you happy. Fun comes in many different forms, but happiness and fulfillment only come in one form: devotion to a loving God and all He stands for. Devotion to God will lead to a lifestyle change. He created us for a deep relationship with Him, so when we go to other things for fulfillment, we will never be filled. If people just drank to have fun, then why would they drink until they are hanging over the toilet vomiting? That's not fun. Hangovers are not fun. Having fun might be part of it, but that's not the main reason people drink.

I started drinking because I was so uncomfortable in my own skin that I needed something to make me different. I did this to the point that when I gave up alcohol I was a totally different person. I drank because I believed I would never fit in with my family. I drank so that I could make decisions I knew were wrong. I drank for so many reasons other than just fun, and so did everyone I knew. We were uncomfortable in who we were, where we came from, and where we were going.

I don't know what God is calling you to today, but whatever it is, it's worth it. The life you believe you're missing out on is nothing more than an illusion. Believe in the goodwill of our God and be obedient. It might mean you're lonely today, but it also might mean you aren't scarred tomorrow. It might mean you're rejected today, but it might mean you're accepted with open arms tomorrow. It's true that God can bring beauty from any pile of ashes, but rising from the ashes is not easy or fun—it's so much better to avoid that type of death.

I have friends who often tell me they wish they had an interesting testimony like mine, wish they could really experience all that grace encompasses. I hope that my complete honesty stops you from believing the lie that those who are faithful to God haven't done anything amazing. I've wished a thousand times that I could trade my abuse of grace and redemption for the quiet strength of a deep and consistent understanding of faithfulness. Remaining faithful to God is much more difficult than giving in. I got to test the waters, but let me be the first to tell you the ride isn't worth the rapids.

CHAPTER 12

GRACE-FILLED SEX

I STILL REMEMBER the first time I heard a preacher talk about sex. I was just coming out of my great rebellion and searching for a Jesus I could really get on board with. I was visiting my oldest brother at a youth camp where he was leading worship, and I loved the talks. We had fun snorkeling in the ocean, and each night I sat with my sister-in-law in the back and watched proudly as my brother pointed thousands of kids to the Lord. When the speakers shared, I wrote furiously in my journal, anxious to learn about my new faith. In true church form, they had a sex talk on the last night of camp. Nothing like a sex talk to get kids all worked up and then send them home to Mom and Dad.

A woman got onstage and started talking about all the reasons why you shouldn't have sex until marriage—the usual dos and don'ts kind of talk. I kept waiting to hear something for the kids who had already screwed up. There was nothing. Not one word. I started to wonder, *Is God's grace not enough for the kids who've already crossed that line? Are you telling me that God's hand is mighty to save but, oh wait, not that mighty?* I left feeling dejected and confused, something I often felt in church. I couldn't help but wonder how many other girls left feeling the same way. How many told themselves, "Well, I guess there's no hope for me"?

That night I decided that if I was ever lucky enough to talk to kids about sex, then I would tell them what people often forget to say—that God's grace is enough, and not only is it enough, but it can wash you clean. If you have already been there and are wondering how you'll ever be whole again, then take heart. God can heal you. Sex outside of marriage is a sin that involves your body. You connect intimately with another person—or in my case, many other people—and it's much harder to heal from. But that doesn't mean Jesus didn't take it to the Cross like everything else. Since nothing can separate you from God, you can fully accept God's grace even after having sex before marriage. He would *never* have left the earth with that kind of outstanding debt. When Jesus was hanging on the cross, the man next to Him, a thief, asked Jesus to remember him in heaven. Jesus didn't hesitate. Instead He said, "I tell you the truth, today you will be with me in paradise" (Luke 23:43).

That is the God we serve. He didn't ask questions. He didn't need a list of sins. He knew that the man had sinned—he was hanging on the cross next to Jesus. And still Jesus assured him a place right with Him. We serve a God so big He can forgive the sins of the world, and sexual sin is no different. Just because you were covered in shame yesterday doesn't mean you can't be smothered in grace today. Walking away from sexual sin is no different than walking away from any other sin. It starts with grace followed by a decision. It's a choice you can make to preserve your heart for your husband. Even if you have already walked down that road, God can make a new path for you.

> Have mercy on me, O God, have mercy on me,
>> for in you my soul takes refuge.
> I will take refuge in the shadow of your wings
>> until the disaster has passed.
> I cry out to God Most High,
>> to God, who fulfills his purpose for me.
> He sends from heaven and saves me,
>> rebuking those who hotly pursue me;
>> God sends his love and his faithfulness.

PSALM 57:1-3

If you have the courage to cry out to God today, He will shelter you while you heal. David wrote this psalm when he was fleeing from Saul, who was searching for him so he could kill him. David hid in a cave and asked God to protect him, and David was never harmed by Saul. You can do the same. You can cry out to the Healer of your broken heart. There may be nothing else you feel you can do, but you can cry out to Him. He will not refuse you grace if you seek it with your whole heart. If you want to be clean, He will make a way for you. Don't believe you can't be healed from this. Jesus came for the sick, not for the healthy. He can be the doctor your heart needs.

God's protection is never more apparent than with baby ducks. They are defenseless. They can barely bite, they are covered in fuzz, and they are perfect snacking size for snakes and turtles. At night, the mother opens up her wings and lets all her babies hide under her soft feathers so that if an enemy comes, the little ducks might have a chance to survive. I never understood the full meaning of the Psalm 57 reference to taking refuge in the shadow of God's wings until I saw a mother duck protect her helpless babies. You and I are the same way. God opens up His huge wings of grace and invites you to come hide under them. He promises that He will fight for you, if you come and rest in His protection.

God does not view sexual sin differently from other sins, but He does warn it is a different type of sin. Sex is unique in that it is the one sin where someone else has control over you. Someone has a piece of you, and you can never have it back. You can be cleansed, purified, and renewed, but a part of your heart will never be returned. I can say this because I have been there.

The fact that I had premarital sex doesn't mean my marriage is doomed, and it doesn't mean that I can't love my husband with everything I have. But it does mean I don't have as much as I once did. It means that I have scars that can never be fully repaired and I have insecurities that cut like a knife to my heart. God tells you not to have sex before marriage for your own good, not for His. Though God may eventually get your whole heart even if you have premarital sex now, what is done cannot be undone. Your heart can be repaired by God, but it was meant to remain whole. One day I'll be whole again. One day I'll stand in front of my Savior, and He will give me the heart I was intended to have. I only wish I could love my husband with that heart. Until then, I'll love my Ben with every part of me. I'll love him with the glued-back-together pieces and know that with God's help, that will be enough.

CHAPTER 13

STARTING OVER AGAIN

LET'S TAKE A look into how God defines love, because I think many girls have bought the same lie that Penny did in *Almost Famous*. We think, *Maybe it is love, as much as it can be.* God defines love very clearly so that we aren't left questioning whether it's love or not. I have a feeling that if you're guessing if it's love, then it's not. You may have heard this before, but read 1 Corinthians 13 now like God is talking to you, like He's sitting across the table from you at Starbucks and is wondering how your relationship with your boyfriend is going. You tell Him things are okay and you're pretty sure it's love. So He asks you . . .

Is he patient? Is he kind? Does he ever lose heart? Does

he give up? Does he get jealous easily? Is he too proud? Does he brag about things that don't matter? Does he get angry easily? Is he rude? Does he seek truth? Does he protect you? Does he trust you? Does he persevere through hard times? Does he remain at your side when life gets tough? Does he put you first? Does he forget the wrong? (See 1 Corinthians 13:4-8.)

You think for a while and realize . . . he doesn't do most of that. At least, not when it doesn't benefit him. I know what you're thinking, because I thought it too: *I'm not worth all that.* Oh, but you are. God, the King of the universe, says you are. These are the standards for love, and God can list them because He does all of them for you. There are God-seeking men out there who love like God loves you.

You must wait for them, just like they should wait until you are that kind of girl. My dad asked me once when I was seventeen if I thought I would marry my boyfriend. I quickly said no, and then he asked me if I was the kind of girl my boyfriend would want to marry. It made me think. Was I? When I did come back to God, I remember thinking that it didn't matter how many lists I made about my requirements in a guy; if I didn't meet the standards of my future husband with a similar list, then he wouldn't be interested. Mr. Perfect isn't interested in good enough—he wants the woman God has prepared for him. So don't expect to get that kind of man until you are that kind of girl.

The passage in 1 Corinthians 13 goes on to say, "When perfection comes, the imperfect disappears. When I was a child, I talked like a child, I thought like a child, I reasoned like a child. When I became a man, I put childish ways behind me" (verses 10-11).

You don't need a boy; you need a God-fearing man. I know this will take time and you will have to wait, but I can promise you it is worth it. I used to believe my brothers were the only God-fearing men on this earth. I believed I would never find anyone as wonderful as they are. I watched how they loved their girlfriends (and then wives), and I was jealous. I figured I would never find a man who could love me like that. My brothers opened doors for their girlfriends, doted on them, respected them, took them on dates, and always, *always* placed God in the center of their relationships. What I saw in them more than anything was that they always put the best interests of their girlfriends before their own best interests. I remember watching that and thinking I had never had a guy who cared more about me than he did about himself.

I knew in high school I would never find a boy like that, because I wasn't being the woman these kind of men go for. But deep down I hoped that one day I'd have the strength to be a God-fearing woman, the kind God-fearing men look for.

Then I met Ben. He was everything and more that I had prayed for, looked for, and heard about. He met every character quality on the list in 1 Corinthians 13, but I only met him after I became God's image of love. I met him after I loved God so deeply that I became like Him. The love Ben and I have for each other is not perfect, but it's as close as you can get. We still fail each other, but we have a standard that our love lives by.

You deserve this. You were made for this. God wants you to know that He deeply desires for you to have this. But if we're putting a standard on our men, then we must also put it on ourselves. So ask yourself the following questions:

Am I patient? Am I kind? Do I get jealous? Do I boast? Am I rude? Do I put myself first? Do I keep a record of wrongs? Do I love truth and pursue it? Do I protect love? Do I trust? Do I hope in love? Do I persevere no matter the cost?

God did. He followed the standard of love set in 1 Corinthians 13 so that you would have the ultimate example of love, because you deserve that kind of love. Don't trade the imitation for the real thing. Don't be Penny Lane and buy the lie that maybe it is love. I can promise you that when you have the real thing, you know it.

If you think you're not good enough, let me assure you, you're *not*. I wasn't; I'm still not. *No one is.* That's why a perfect Savior came down and died, so He could save you from human standards, so He could save you from the evil of this world and replace it with something new: a new identity, a new life, and a new standard that you deserve. You are a daughter of the King, and you deserve to be treated as such.

Jesus has a different kind of love to offer you, one that can only be displayed on a cross. It's not a dozen roses, but it's a gift that keeps on giving. You don't have to say anything to win Him over, because He has already been fighting for you. We tend to look at His love through human eyes, and we question it: What can You give me in this life, right now, to make the decision to follow You worth it? It's a shrewd question, but the question it's really asking is, what can you give me today? You weigh the pros and cons, and at first you may say, "Not too much." But God's love was never aimed at only the here and now; He was aiming for forever. Then you look at gifts that last forever, and they are amazing. Even though He can offer you a lot today, His goal was to offer you everything forever. Yes, He can provide you comfort and a future, but there's so much more. He wants to give you paradise. This is just the first date; the really good stuff comes later.

God's love is never faulty, and ours is. God's love is never selfish, and ours is. God doesn't rely on a feeling to know He loves us, but rather a painful choice He made to win our hearts. If we count on this type of love to fill us, understanding that no human will ever be able to offer what God can, then we can rest in His love and love others with His power. What if we changed our dating lens to find the man who loves God the most, instead of the one who makes us feel the best? What if we always had in mind that God loves us completely? If we were already full, I daresay we might not be nearly as needy. We might be able to rest instead of constantly searching for someone to love us. No matter how great Mr. Right is, he will never love you like Jesus does. He can't.

When we are full, our love for God becomes so enriched by His love that we can pour into others instead of sucking them dry. That's what I did in relationships: I got in and sucked the love out of the other person. I took their hugs, kisses, and kind words and bottled them up to drink, and it gave me "life." Each day I drank in the potion that was running me dry. And the more I drank, the more I needed. This is how most of us feel, dry from pouring ourselves out to others, dry from the addictions that never satisfy, dry from the pain people have fed us. Our hearts have become deserts, and the Lord longs to bring in a river, soaking our hearts' depths. A river of love that can be given and not only taken, love that will quench the thirst we've been trying to fill for the ages. The question still remains, though: Can it be done?

I didn't think it could. I was so dependent on what I could get from others that I believed I could never be satisfied. I had sucked the life out of relationships, friends, and family and was still thirsty. Then I met my Savior, and something happened. He filled me. It didn't seem natural, but it was satisfying. It took effort, but it lasted. It called for sacrifices, but I was healed. He asked me to pour out myself so that I could be filled with Him, and He never failed me.

I realized that I wanted so desperately for it to be true—the verses I read describing His love. A love I couldn't wrap my hands around or mold into my own image, one that is unable to be lost. Even if I couldn't feel the depths of the statement, I hoped with everything in me that God could love me despite my many faults, because I'd never felt that. Every love I knew had been shattered by human frailty, so I doubted there was a power greater than my own mishaps. For a time, I had tried to fight this love. I had spat in its face, hammered nails through its limbs, ripped flesh from its back, crowned it with thorns, all the while mocking its name, but His love grew deeper as my pain grew stronger.

Suddenly, full force, it hit me like a rock: I can't run from the deep, everlasting love of a Savior who takes my shame and pronounces me dearly loved. The words from 1 Corinthians strike at my core because I was created to be loved that much. He came and died so I would have something tangible, something that shouts at me, "You are loved this much." If you really believe that, you will behave differently. If you can really grasp this, then suddenly you're worth so much more than you ever believed possible.

His love never gives up on you. Crown Him with pain; He will still hang for you. Nail Him to wood, and the Son of God will beg forgiveness on your behalf. We may not have been there on that hill the day Jesus died, and we may not have held the hammer, but time and time again we have poured salt on His wounds when we've said to God, "Your love isn't enough." God's design for your life makes an impact because it's so different from what you've been told about your life. Satan tells you that you don't deserve a love that travels to the depths of your heart, but God says differently. He forever holds you—and me—in His hands, never to fall, because you're the beloved and you're to be loved.

When You Least Expect It

January 13

You never know the nights that are going to change your life. You wonder when they'll happen, and you dream about the possibilities of a chance meeting, a great conversation, or a new friend, but you never know. That's the beauty of life, the mystery of tomorrow. While it all sounds romantic, the truth is most days are just regular, normal days. They continue at the same pace, time doesn't stop, and monotony becomes a part of the routine until there's a bend in the road, and suddenly life changes.

The night I met my husband didn't announce itself. As I was getting ready to go out, I had no idea this was the night I'd meet the man I'd been praying for. I'd gone to a movie with friends, finally done the laundry, and was looking forward to going to a party with a friend. I didn't think anything out of the ordinary would happen. I'd given up on the notion of love and Prince Charming. I'd stopped believing in fairy tales, accepting that most knights were just regular men who were better at hiding their true natures. So I didn't go into the night with the idea of meeting him. But I did.

I noticed him from across the room, and my heart did a double take. He was laughing with his friends, and something about his broad smile caught me off guard. Once I noticed him, I couldn't stop staring, never expecting he would talk to me. For a second, he caught me watching him, and I smiled before I could stop myself. Then I stared at the ground.

I still don't know exactly why he chose to come up to me, but he did. We began talking and didn't stop until the party was over. We shared stories and laughed, and while I watched him smile, I prayed that the night would never end. In a sense, it didn't. When my friends and I left the party, I said a silent good-bye to the mystery man, accepting that we'd probably never meet again, but I couldn't help wondering who he was. I found myself keenly interested in a stranger whose name I didn't even know.

It's been several years since that night, and we're madly in love. I can't take a breath without thinking about him, and we're planning a future that includes each other. Before him, I gave up on true love; I never dreamed God would give me the desires of my heart. Then Ben walked into my life and renewed my confidence in love and helped show me that God does want the best for me. I realized then why God had asked me to wait: because he had something better in mind.

I always imagined love like this, the kind that affects every area of your life. It overflows into your smile and speaks to you without saying anything. When I was younger, I used to lie in bed and dream about the day I would meet him. Now that it's happened, it's even more romantic than my best fairy tale. It's a story of a chance meeting that turned into something amazing. It was a regular Saturday night; I never planned to find him.

We both knew that this was it, and the closer we got, the more we disclosed. I had to tell him about my scarred past, and he had to accept that he had waited on someone who hadn't had the same kind of patience. It was something Satan loved to run with. He would tempt us to make the same mistakes together, because, after all, I'd given myself to far less worthy men. He tempted Ben to walk away for someone with a more virtuous past. No matter how much good God has been able to do with my past, it's still there begging to become a wound in our relationship.

April 16

Four months and twenty-seven days until my wedding, and I realize I've never had an HIV test. Ben brought it up after reading an article about HIV in America. Suddenly my world is turned upside down, fear pulsates in each heartbeat: if only I'd considered today when I made my decisions of yesterday. Fear had no place in my life when I decided to sleep with my longtime boyfriend. I was as invincible as every seventeen-year-old is. I didn't consider the possibility that someday I'd meet Ben and have to explain why I gave my body away so carelessly. For so many years I'd been told not to have sex, but not how to handle passion. Maybe if I'd envisioned today, I'd have chosen differently. When most girls are worrying about wedding dresses and flower colors, I'm scheduling an HIV test that will decide my future. It will decide whether I have kids or not and whether I continue with my wedding. Five years later, I'm still crying for my mistakes. No amount of redemption can change my past decisions, and no amount of forgiveness can change the

consequences. I'm praying my past doesn't dictate my
future, that I get to have my happily ever after, that I
didn't ruin my marriage for a few beers and one big,
bad decision.

This is the sex story you never hear; the movies tend to leave out this part. The couple is always quick to jump into bed, but the movie doesn't show the unromantic parts that follow that passionate night. Maybe if teens got a greater dose of the reality of sex, they would realize it's not quite the fairy tale they've imagined. The movies never show you at the doctor's office taking a test that will decide your future. They never show you in a puddle of tears, regret spilling from your eyes. So I'll tell you, this is the honest side of sex, the side that comes when you give your body away for some fun on Friday night. It might not affect you greatly now, but there will come a time when it will creep up on you and try to rip your future from your hands. It will try to take the happiness you were meant to have.

A few weeks later, I went to the doctor to get an HIV test. I was shaking as the nurse drew blood. They told me they would call me in a few days. I waited for what seemed like forever for them to call, and when I saw the voice mail, I listened with anticipation. I asked my mom to call the nurse back since I was at work, and a wave of relief washed over me as she told me I was not HIV positive. I would get to have my happily ever after, after all.

All this could have been prevented, though, and not just by my using a condom. It could have been prevented by my not having sex, and *that* might have been delayed, made less frequent, or maybe avoided altogether if I'd known more. Not more cold facts and statistics, more of the emotional reality. Things might have been different if I'd been told about the pain that comes with premarital sex, if someone had told me about the look your future spouse gets when you tell him you haven't waited. Maybe things could have been different if someone had told me that once you cross that line with one boy, it's hard to go back.

Truthfully, I don't know if my mind could have been changed, because the passion was just as real as the pain that followed. The feelings were real even if they weren't real love. The challenge is that while the feelings are real, they are fleeting, and the pain that follows is not. What I really wish had been conveyed to me is that the consequences far outweigh the momentary benefits.

Sex is embarrassing to talk about, but sitting in a doctor's office asking for an HIV test months before your wedding is worse. The emotional emptiness of casual sex is gut wrenching, but the physical danger is terrifying. Don't miss this: there is a lot more to sex than what society may show you or what your parents are willing or able to share. The movies only show a small portion, and magazines play up how-to advice and play down the emotional emptiness and the scary STD stats. Sex has many sides, and some of them you don't want to see.

Sex and Marriage

Marital sex is laced with something that can never happen with couples who are just dating: commitment, commitment, commitment. The way I see it, there are three components that distinguish marital sex from premarital sex, and these three components can't be had outside of marriage. They are unconditional love that comes with commitment, physical attraction that doesn't fade with time because of commitment, and the promise to never leave because you've made a commitment. Now, I understand that while I write this almost half the people who've been married in this country have gone through a divorce, but I don't have the knowledge or wisdom to get into that. I just know what I have experienced and what God has shown me. Yes, the world is broken and marriages are not all healthy, but I believe God designed marriages to be quite different and that God designed sex for marital commitment.

The reason that commitment is such a *huge* part of sex is because you're making yourself vulnerable to someone and asking him to love you. You can only be sure he will once you've proclaimed to the world that you will love no one else but this person and he has done the same. I'm not saying that marriages don't have flaws and that they don't end, but that doesn't make premarital sex any more lasting. The old adage stands true: two wrongs don't make a right.

Let me give you the key to why I think most men want to have sex before marriage (I'm not talking about the ones who may have made a mistake; I'm talking about the guys who flat out say, "I don't want to wait until marriage to have sex.") Here is the key. It's really simple, and I'm sure you don't want to believe me, but that won't make it any less true. Ready?

He wants to have sex with you because he wants love, just like you. And just like you, he has a need that he was created with. But also like you, he doesn't know what will fill that need. So he goes to you with his heart in the hopes that you might make him feel a certain way, or not feel a certain way. But the truth is if he really cared about you, if he really thought about what was best for you, then he would know that sex before marriage is not in your best interest. The consequences of premarital sex far outweigh the moments of pleasure, and if he really cared about your heart, if he was really a man like God says you deserve, he would know that sex should come with a lasting commitment. Same goes for you: if you really care about him, if you really love him, then you will be more concerned with his best interest than meeting your needs. See, guys have gotten a bad rap for not wanting to wait, but I think the same is true of girls. You can't truly love someone that

God has called you to love and think sex outside of marriage is a good idea. It can't be justified; the consequences are too great.

You can dress up premarital sex in fancy words and justify it with the need to have a physical connection, but it all boils down to one thing. When you strip it down to its nakedness, you'll find this is at the core: one of you doesn't truly have the other's best interest at heart, and Christian or not, I think most of us can agree that real love puts the other first. Truth is, premarital sex is very selfish and really about one or both of you only wanting what you want—your needs met. I like to eat dessert before dinner. I don't much like real food; I just like sugar, so I cheat and eat the dessert before I get my protein. Why? Because it tastes good. Wanting sex before marriage is like wanting dessert without dinner. Sex is a benefit of marriage, not a right. Marriage is not defined by sex. Sex, on the other hand, is made for marriage alone. A lot of people think of sex as a right, like freedom of speech or something. Sex is a pleasure; you won't die without it (contrary to popular opinion), and sex is not something that's owed to you. Because God created it as a bonus to marriage, it cannot be truly enjoyed with a completely free and trusting heart unless it comes with marriage.

Commitment might not feel like that big of a deal, but let me promise you that when it comes to sex, it is a huge deal. Every high school has that couple where the girl is dating a good-for-nothing guy: he cheats, he's a drunk, and he treats her like junk, but for some reason she can't leave him. Every time they break up, it lasts about one day before they are canoodling in the halls again. Why? If I had to guess, I'd say sex is at the root of the attachment issue. She is attached to him and therefore can't give him up. Each time she leaves him, she feels part of her heart go with him, and so she goes back for it. He couldn't care less—he knows she'll come back, even though everyone is looking on, telling her to drop him like a bad habit. Everyone else can see it so clearly; why can't she? She can't because he has a part of her. To make things worse, to literally add insult to injury, she acts like a fool for him, begging him to take her back, giving herself away like something you get out of a vending machine.

I know because I was her. I couldn't shake a relationship that was no good for me. I couldn't leave him because he had a part of me that would never be returned. No matter what I did to move on, my heart was in his hands, and the only way I could have it back was by being with him. I thought I would never be whole again. I knew deep down that I was making decisions and doing things I'd always said I would never do, but the emotional draw to him clouded my thinking. Everything I did was filtered through this need to get my heart back.

Then I met Jesus. He replaced the parts of me that were missing with His own beating heart. He sewed the pieces in carefully. When I couldn't walk, He carried me. When I wanted to let go, He held my hand. And when I wanted to run back to get the lost parts of me, He offered me something better. He offered me satisfaction and true love.

It didn't make sense. I could offer Him nothing, but He gave me everything. I can still feel the scars some days, when an old song comes on or when I hear the loud cheering at football games. I can never forget the broken shape Jesus found me in. But He didn't leave me that way; He turned a deserted girl into a redeemed woman. I traded rags for riches, ashes for beauty, and brokenness for a whole heart.

I call sex in the confines of marriage sacred sex. It's my way of separating the pain I experienced with sex from the joy I now have in marital sex. There is a great difference between the two, and it's far worth the wait. Before I got married, I had to go through a lot of counseling to be able to distinguish between the two, and I'm glad to report that once again God did miraculous things.

Sometimes parents ask me how to prevent their teenage daughters from having sex before marriage. My advice to parents is to tell their daughters to think about having to tell their future husbands all the things they did with someone who will later mean nothing to them. When you sleep with your future husband, you're bringing to bed everything from your past—all the abuse, neglect, pain, hurt, and lies.

But you have a choice. You can make the decision now to say no and save yourself for sacred sex.

> Listen, O daughter, consider and give ear:
>> Forget your people and your father's house.
> The king is enthralled by your beauty;
>> honor him, for he is your lord.

PSALM 45:10-11

CHAPTER 14

THROUGH MY MIRROR

If you could see yourself through My mirror
You wouldn't grab at your sides or complain about
your smile
Your eyes wouldn't be too big or small
And your features would be worthwhile
You would brag about how your butt looks in jeans
No matter how big the size may seem
You wouldn't find the fat you hate
Or every reason to try and lose weight

If you would take a look through My eyes
Your body wouldn't be your greatest fear
Or a goal that repeats every new year

You wouldn't spend hours primping
Only to complain about your curls now limping
The gym would be a thing of the past
And diet ice cream would never last

Dear daughter, you must have forgotten
In My eyes you have no flaws
Each curve was constructed, each eye was placed
When I put you together My heart began to race
Beautiful daughter of the King, won't you listen,
     won't you come near
You are the crown of creation I long to hold dear
There are no mistakes, no marks I don't know
I formed you with neatness and care to show
You are My beauty reflected on earth
No sunset can depict how much you are worth
So smile proud for your Father, the Creator
He finds you worthy; He holds you high and wants
     you to see
See through the eyes of the King

So take a look with Me again at the mirror
Let Me fade into your beauty and watch the image
     become clearer

Your beauty should not come from outward
adornment, such as braided hair and the wearing

of gold jewelry and fine clothes. Instead, it should be that of your inner self, the unfading beauty of a gentle and quiet spirit, which is of great worth in God's sight.

I PETER 3:3-4

I was twenty years old when I felt God calling me to give back to Him. He was calling me to serve at the youth camp that had been so instrumental (now that I look back on it!) in my teen years. Kristian had led worship there, and I already knew I loved the camp, so I applied to be an intern. I went into the summer knowing I'd be working long days running the small details of the camp. I was ready, though. At the beginning of the summer, the interns and employees took a trip to Africa, and I was eager to see how the rest of the world lived. After we went to Africa, we came back to Florida to set up for camp and to get ready for the twelve hundred kids who would come through each week.

It was the hardest work I'd ever done, but God showed up in huge ways. It was the first time I shared my testimony since recommitting my life to Christ. I spent a lot of time with kids who were just like me. I put my sweat and tears into the camp and got more out of it than I ever believed possible. I saw the Lord use my broken past to help other girls like me. It was a great summer, but it was also very trying. I was working eighteen-hour days on little sleep and got injured very early on in my time there. I had to fly home and get cortisone shots in my hip. I took an hour off a week for physical therapy, but because I was unwilling to give up a lot of my time with the kids, I didn't get the rest I needed. Every day we woke up at six and got ready. We had an intern meeting, followed by the morning session. The interns ran the cameras, controlled the lights, worked the store, and basically served the kids who came through each week.

That was still a summer of recovery for me. At the end of camp, the leaders took each intern aside to give them encouragement and, if needed, criticism. I was ready for some vital encouragement after fully committing my life to this camp. I'd given everything I had, and I desperately wanted to hear that my work was good. When my turn came, the leaders of the camp told me I'd done a great job, but then they said something that stunned me. They said I would always have to rise above my beauty. They told me I'd be taken advantage of because I was a beautiful girl and that I would constantly be fighting circumstances I hadn't created. I walked out of the meeting and almost cried. That was all they could tell me after months of backbreaking work? That my beauty would get in the way of my cause? I was in shock. It was the first time I realized how much I resented how other people saw me. I hated that they might be right, that for the rest of my life I would have to fight against some stereotype. And it hurt that after all I'd given, this was what they'd focused on.

I wanted to be taken seriously, and I should have been. I trusted these leaders to see beyond the physical. I wanted to be given the kind of encouragement I so desperately needed. More than anything else, I wanted them to recognize that God was working in my life. On that day, my past became more real than ever before. The leaders at the Christian youth camp had just taught me something I'd never forget: some people will only take you at face value and will never look deeper. And the people who taught me this were Christians.

This challenged everything I thought about becoming a Christian. I thought I was leaving the past behind me, moving on to bigger and better things. Instead, the same struggles were present in my Christian life. I was actually doing something with my life, but all the leaders could see was what appeared to be a pretty face. It was a blow I didn't forget, and even now I wonder if they were right. I wonder how I would have been treated if I'd been Inker from the middle school class. When she came to me asking if she could show me her heart and soul, I listened and found a way to support her. If I'd looked like Inker, acted like Inker, demanded their attention like Inker, would they have looked past my appearance and instead seen beauty and courage in my work?

The truth is, there are times when beauty can feel like more of a burden than a blessing. If you're attractive, you're constantly praised for being so. Sometimes it's as if that's all you have to offer. But if you aren't told you're beautiful, if you don't hear that kind of praise, you'll do anything to get it. As a woman, you have so much more to offer the world than just your appearance. Okay, maybe some of you look great doing your work, but that's not what you're here for. God's design for your beauty is to express a part of Himself that isn't generally expressed in men. And He made you uniquely beautiful among women. Think about the most beautiful place you've ever been. Didn't you look at it and think, *How can there not be a God?*

Women are a representation of the beauty that God is, and while some of the world may tell you one thing because of your hair, or your eyes, or your skin, or your size, God looks at you and sees that you are perfect—your whole package. If the world has been telling you something besides that, then take heart in 1 John 5:19: "The whole world is under the control of the evil one," which means that anything this world has told you isn't true. The truth is, God believes you're beautiful and He has made you in His image just as you are. He created vast oceans, tree-topped mountains, and flowers that can fill a field, but when He made *you*, He said you were "fearfully and wonderfully made" (Psalm 139:14).

Women have a unique struggle to not let our looks define us. Beauty is not all you have to offer the world or men. You are unique in your perspectives, opinions, and in what you can do for the Lord. We were created for more than just being looked at, and yet we scrutinize one another brutally, we judge and are judged by our appearance far more than we like to admit. I feel Satan has an easy time attacking women, because for the most part we're an insecure bunch, constantly trying to lose weight, look taller (or for me, shorter), or whatever else. The worst part is we egg each other on. Could you imagine what your friends would say if during a body-bashing session you said, "I think I look pretty good"? They'd stare at you in awe and then talk about you for the next few weeks. We have this ideal that's unreachable. Society pushes it, and we drink it in along with cleanses, flushes, and diet pills. Our appearance is constantly thought about, talked about, and criticized, so we grow up learning that we're imperfect, that all that matters is how good we look in our new jeans. I am telling you, God made you for so much more. He created your beauty as an asset, not the be-all and end-all.

At seventeen, however, I had to be seen as attractive, and to be seen as attractive, I believed I had to be desired by men. To prove that I was desired by men, I thought I had to give my body away. There were countless times I drank until I almost passed out and found myself in bed with an undeserving guy. I woke up with guilt, feeling more alone than when the night had started. I didn't value my body, so I wore clothes that sent a clear message to "look all you want."

Today it's even easier for girls to send that message: a quick picture and you can send your body via Internet. It breaks my heart that this is the new trend, boys getting the benefit without any of the commitment. I have to think that God is weeping at each click, each time you value yourself as nothing more than a piece of media. I don't care who's doing it, how easy it is, or if you believe it means nothing. You're worth more than a media message; you're worth the lavished love of a King. You're His queen, come to earth to display His loving beauty and deep relational heart. You're worth more than Friday night drunken make-outs, one-night stands, and dirty picture messages. You are worth the King of the world giving His only Son to be killed in the most painful way possible for a chance to be with you. Can you see that? Jesus came and died to have a relationship with you. It wasn't because you look good in a miniskirt or because you can roll a cherry stem into a knot with your tongue; it's because of who you are. Maybe that's scary to you, because you don't know who you are; you've spent your life giving away your body because you believed it was all you had to offer. Beloved, listen to me: that isn't even the tip of the iceberg of what you have to offer. Your beauty is an outward reflection of God's beautiful work inside you. Your complex heart was made by Him to fill with joy each time you love God enough to respect yourself.

My need to give myself away came from a desire to be known at a level that I could really feel. I wanted to be appreciated for who I was and thought if I could hook guys in with my body, then they would come to love me. That wasn't true. Most guys were never interested in any more than what I could offer them for a night. A few of the good ones were, but there was still the expectation of a physical relationship. They were interested in me as long as I'd fulfill their needs when night came. So these guys would be left seemingly satisfied while I was left bruised, wondering why I couldn't find anyone who loved me. I was looking in all the wrong places. One-night stands do not turn into lasting relationships; I don't care what he told you in the moment.

I know what you believe, because I believed it once too. You think it's not a big deal, everyone's having sex, he really loves you, or maybe you don't care whether or not he loves you. Maybe you just want to be loved night by night, feeling that you will gain something each time you give yourself away. It is hurting you, though; you are losing precious pieces of your heart, usually to someone who is unworthy. Once again, sex is a sin that promises instant gratification, but in order to gain it you sacrifice long-term satisfaction. What I didn't realize is that God knows me. Psalm 139 says He watches everything we do and He searches our hearts, not our faces, to see our desires.

The following verses from Ezekiel are about the nation of ancient Israel and how the people disregarded God despite all He had done for them. But I believe the passage

also provides a picture of what God can do for our mishandled beauty. I've phrased it here to reflect the way these
verses translated in my life.

> I saw the way you were exposing your body,
> and I covered your nakedness with my cloak. I
> took your shame and cleaned your broken heart;
> I cleaned your cuts and dressed your wounds. I
> put you in a beautiful dress and adorned you with
> beautiful jewels. I placed a crown on your head
> and lifted you up to your rightful place as my
> queen. Your beauty caused the earth to talk of my
> splendor, and I made you perfect. Your beauty
> became an outward adornment in a world of
> gloom. All who looked at you could see the deep
> love of a Father.
>
> EZEKIEL 16:8-14 (PARAPHRASED)

What if we really believed this—that God has taken
our shame onto Himself and made us clean and righteous?
For me, the word *righteous* seems far too dignified. I know
what I've done with my body and the people I've hurt with
my words, and "righteous" is much too big for me. I did
nothing to deserve my righteousness, but God did everything so that I could have it.

We can choose to accept His gift of righteousness,
though, but many times we don't. I was so convinced I had

to be righteous before I accepted God's grace that I spent years obsessing over the rules. The point is, if we are waiting to deserve the gift God has given us, we will never deserve it. If we are waiting until the gift is rightfully ours, we will end up burying it in the dirt and never recovering it. God has given you a beautiful gift, not because you deserve it but because He loves you and He loves to lavish you with presents. Isn't it better when you can look someone in the eye and truly say, "I don't deserve this"? That makes the gift all the more special. God is holding out a precious gift to you, and if you wait to take it until you clean up your life or get all the rules right, I promise the crown will grow dusty in His hands. He never asks us to clean up our lives to find Him. He just says we need to call out to Him, and He will be there.

God doesn't think your struggle is silly, and He knows you're beautiful, but He also knows your true beauty won't come from this world. He places things inside you to make you beautiful through Him. I might have known how to wear a low-cut shirt when I was seventeen, but I knew nothing about the beauty God could give me. I was a selfish person, caught up in what I could get from people and who I could use. I was brash and unrelenting in my opinions. After I gave my heart over to Christ, I felt like the Grinch at the end of the story, when his heart grows three sizes. God gave me a love for others and softened my heart. He turned my cynicism into compassion and my brashness into boldness for His cause. I became a beautiful person inside, and I didn't have to sleep with anyone to attain this.

I'm sure there are plenty of people who only know God for the beauty He has created. They look at the world around them, and they say, "What a beautiful God." And you know what? All the while God is saying, "There's so much more to Me than just My beauty."

As women, we know this! There is more to God than the beauty He created, just like there is more to us than our beauty. Maybe we have to spend our lives overcoming what people see, but that doesn't mean we can't do it. I went into that summer with seventeen other interns, and they all saw my picture and immediately thought I was going to be a lazy sorority girl who expected everyone to work for her. (They admitted this to me later.) Some of the guys were rude to me because they assumed I wouldn't be willing to work. They made fun of my preppy clothes and the fact that I brought a straightener to Africa and blew a fuse that caused the whole hotel to lose power (okay, maybe I deserved being made fun of a little). But at the end of the summer, I'd earned the respect of eleven doubting guys. I showed them I could work hard and that I had things to add to the group *because* I was a woman, not in spite of the fact that I was a woman.

Esther was chosen to be queen on the basis of her beauty, but while on the throne she saved God's people.

She changed the fate of a people because of her character (see the book of Esther). Beauty is a gift just like any other quality, but it is not what defines you, just like your ability to play a sport doesn't make you who you are. Your beauty is an asset that will bring God glory, but so is your kindness, your intelligence, your willingness to work, your fairness, your courage, and your humility. When He looks into your soul, He sees all of you, and that is beautiful.

Did you know that whenever God talks about wisdom in the Bible, He uses a feminine pronoun? It's a little reminder of how much God thinks of our gender.

> Wisdom calls aloud in the street,
> 　*she* raises *her* voice in the public squares;
> at the head of the noisy streets *she* cries out,
> 　in the gateways of the city *she* makes *her* speech:
> "How long will you simple ones love your simple
> 　ways?"
>
> PROVERBS 1:20-22 (EMPHASIS ADDED)

When God sees us, He doesn't just see a pretty face; He sees a voice of wisdom, a heart of compassion, and a spirit of strength. What if we rose to the occasion and started living as the women He created us to be? Think about what we could do for the world if we started taking women at more than face value? I don't care what the world has told you about who you are and what you bring to the table, the King of the world calls you beautiful and full of wisdom. What greater compliment is there?

Wisdom takes time and understanding. It doesn't mean you aren't going to make a few mistakes along the way. It means you pursue truth and righteousness instead of things that fade.

Sometimes the wisest thing you can do is say no. I know that today "no" is often considered taboo, but there will come a time when you find that you have to deny some of your senses. But sometimes wisdom is saying no to things you really want. Yes, sin feels good, tastes good, and looks good. I have wished so many times that I could go back and refuse—refuse the shot, the drink, the joint, the urge to do whatever I wanted. But I can't go back. I have to live with all those yeses. You don't have to, though.

I grew up in a house full of boys and a beautiful mom. I was never great at things like cotillion, and I could burp louder than any of my brothers. I played in the mud. When my grandparents gave me a Barbie, it became a dog toy. This is probably why I didn't really understand girls; they would say one thing and mean something else. Don't get me wrong—I learned quickly that I was supposed to lie to my friends' faces and then talk behind their backs, fight over boys who didn't matter, and so on. I never really got it, though. Why couldn't we just be honest or at least say nothing at all? Estrogen really screwed me up; it made me feel things I didn't want to. It made me crazy at least one week out of the month and in pain for another week. Before my husband and I got married, he said, "So we really only have half of our life together since one week is dedicated to PMS and the other to your period?" That just doesn't seem fair to me. Then I realized it's not.

It took me a long time to come to grips with the burdens I hold as a woman. I'm in no way diminishing a man's struggle, because I have no way to compare the two. But for a long time I resented that men seemed to have an easier time of everything. They don't have periods or PMS, they don't get pregnant, they aren't scrutinized for physical perfection the way we are, and their reputations aren't nearly as tarnished as ours when they give in to temptation. But then I realized this resentment prevented me from using my gift of wisdom. This was the lie Satan wanted me to believe. If he could have me believe that God had dealt me a harder hand than the other half of the population, then he could distract me from so many things. He could induce anger toward God and my husband, and he could do what he really sets out to do, which is distract me from God's calling. For a while, I really bought it. I weighed the problems of both genders and thought, *Heck, a period alone takes the cake*, but the more I thought about it, the more I realized it doesn't really matter. I finally talked to my dad and told him what I was thinking. His response was, "Say you do have it harder. That doesn't change what will make you happy." And it doesn't.

The important thing to hear is that we do not serve a sexist God. Perhaps He gave females a greater burden because He knew we could handle it. Or perhaps it's not greater at all, and I'm blinded by my PMS. Or maybe it's all Eve's fault (told you I got the hang of being a girl!). In any case, God is not sexist, and He is also not male. Yes, Jesus was a man, but God created both man and woman *in His own image*. Therefore, He cannot simply be a man; He is gender neutral.

I think Satan would love it if women discarded the Bible just because we wanted to prove a point, because we wanted to show the world we don't need some book written by men who don't understand us. The Bible is full of women— important women. Jesus made it to earth through Mary; perhaps the greatest picture of love was given to us by Mary (the sister of Martha) when she anointed Jesus' feet with her nicest perfume; and so the list goes on. The Bible is filled with influential women who made a great cause for Christ. A lot of women are more relational, just like God. We were given an innate ability to take care of others, to show the world God's beauty, to have deep relationships, to be wise in tough situations, and more. God has entrusted us with great things, which means we will have great burdens. The classic line in *Spider-Man* is "with great power comes great responsibility." We have great power; therefore, we have great responsibilities.

Since we're often more in tune with our emotions than

men, we may feel more deeply than most men do. I find it interesting that women seek treatment for depression more often than men. Is it because we feel too much? Hurt too much for others? Take on so much in one day? Or is it simply that we have a greater sense that this world is falling apart? We carry so much on our shoulders and often have a hard time giving that burden to God. I know this because it's one of my greatest faults. I'm not satisfied unless I have my hand in at least four things. I don't like a whole lot of idle time, so I fill my days until I'm so stressed I get sick and depressed. I turn away from God's help because I feel I should change the world all on my own, even though He never asked me to do so. I want to prove that being a woman won't hold me back, even if I don't know who I'm trying to prove something to. God created me exactly as I am to fulfill something for His Kingdom. Let me repeat that: God created me *exactly* as I am. Even though I might not want to accept the burdens that come with being a woman, I'm who God made me to be, and He did it with His glory in mind. You were designed to bring glory to God. Don't forget that fact as you strive to prove something to this world.

The fall after I worked so relentlessly at the Christian youth camp, I came home to find that I wasn't the same person as when I left. The world didn't look the same as it had a few months earlier, and some days it was hard to even get out of bed. Every night I lay in bed wide awake and prayed that sleep would come. I didn't want to go out with my friends or even be in a room with people. I started to feel like no one understood the hectic summer I'd had or why it had taken such a toll on my body or why my botched review mattered so much to me. Shortly after I got back, the relationship I was in at the time went downhill. I realized something was terribly wrong. I talked to my mom about the overwhelming sadness I was feeling daily and how I couldn't seem to shake it. My mom knew what was going on, because she'd experienced the same feelings. She urged me to go to the doctor, so after a few months I finally did. I was quickly diagnosed with depression. It was a huge blow for me. I'd always prided myself on being so strong, and I saw my depression as a sign of weakness instead of what it really was—an illness.

Most of us don't like feeling vulnerable, but sometimes as women we do. Normally, we're perfectly safe, but at times we experience fear, knowing the statistics and worrying that we'll be attacked because of our gender. Just like there are times we have to look above and say how great our God is, there are many times when we can't deny that Satan is alive and well. Every time we hear of another rape, suicide, shooting, death, or kidnapping, we know that the king of lies has deceived again. It's on days like these that we need to know how great our God is. It's times like these that God will remain good in our eyes only when we remember who to blame for evil. We often look around our perverted world and want to shake our fists at God. We hear of another hurting nation and ask, "God, where are You?" He sits where He has always sat, in heaven weeping for the people He created to live with. Separated by a barrier of sin, He has to watch as the course of time takes its toll on our world. Satan will be strong until God's plan for earth is complete. Until then, Satan wants our world to suffer as he has to suffer. So he convinces people to act as he would see fit. Satan is the ultimate example of misery loving company.

Who is Satan? What is he? He is the father of all lies. He is a walking metaphor for all aspects of evil. He's the voice in your head telling you that you'll never be enough. He's the whispering fears that rise up every time you forget the truth. He is the great deceiver, and he preys on the downtrodden. Satan is the greatest evil this world will ever know. He loves destruction and death, he loves pain and suffering, and he laughs in the face of the brokenhearted. Satan loves when his lies make you doubt the one true God. He loves twisting truth. He is jealous and angry, and his only desire is your life. He will say anything to you to convince you that God is against you. He seizes on your greatest fears about yourself and tells you they're all true. He tempts all of us who walk this earth to leave our beloved Savior for a life of earthly pleasure. He knows this will never satisfy, so he wants to trap you in the chains of sin so tightly that you can't see your way out. He wants to place you in a pit so deep that the top seems miles away, and all the while he will tell you that this is what you want. His lies are convincing and self-gratifying. His plan of attack is the simple fact that your soul craves what this world has to offer. The lie is that it will make you happy. He tells you that you need to be more, have more, and want more.

Satan is not simply a fallen angel. He is the angel who wanted to be worshiped above God. He isn't a puppy with sharp claws. He is a roaring lion waiting to devour. His attack isn't with sticks and stones but with a bullet straight to your heart. He isn't the man in a red suit who sits on your shoulder and tells you to eat the cake. He is the evil in the night with plenty who do his bidding. He isn't a ghost story or a myth. He is the worst nightmare you have ever had and the darkest moment of your life. He is powerful, and he is the king of all things evil. He wants to see you destroyed.

Just the other day, I heard another shocking story—one of my parents' friends took his own life and that of his wife. My heart broke a little bit. I don't know this person or the family, but I know that Satan has wreaked havoc in their lives. Part of me wanted to blame God, but then I remembered God only desires good for our lives. He doesn't cause bad. He tearfully allows it so that we may have our free will. If news seems to grow worse, it's because each day Satan gets a little closer to his death.

Never doubt that God is watching, though. He hurts like we hurt, and His tears are laced with the sins of this world. Like a father weeps for a lost child, our God weeps for a lost world. He made a way for us to be with Him, but only if we choose it. He will never force a heart to turn to Him, because He desires our sincerity, and let me tell you, there is nothing more sincere than having a heart renewed by God. So when you're tempted, like me, to look around and ask God where He is, remember He is with you in your sorrow and also in your triumphs. He is with the dying and the brokenhearted, and just because we refuse Him access doesn't mean He won't stand with us and weep. God triumphs in good, but He also triumphs over evil, in His perfect time.

CHAPTER 15

SOMETHING TO BELIEVE IN

MY OLDEST BROTHER always had a way of making me believe that God had great plans for me. Even when I was in the midst of trouble or knee deep in sin, he would look me in the eyes and tell me, "Tindell, God is going to do great things in your life." I tried to brush it off like I did everything else, but for some reason his words stuck with me. He believed in me when he shouldn't have, and he didn't give up on me even though all the odds seemed stacked against his faith in me. He knew this was just a phase of my life and not how my life would end. He knew one day God would turn my trials into glory for His name. There's no mistaking God's work. He takes pain, heartache, and rejection and turns them into great things for His Kingdom. Loneliness will turn into longing for Him, which will turn into a deeper relationship with Him and with others.

Alcohol abuse and addiction turn into redemption, which turns into compassion for others, which turns into the spreading of hope. Ugly circumstances turn into great testimonies. There doesn't seem to be anything greater than a testimony of hope, a life transformed by a great God.

We're coming up on Easter as I write this, a time of remembering what Jesus has done for us, and at church on Sunday people came out with big poster boards that read, "I remember . . ." with a portion of their lives described on the front. When they flipped the boards over, the boards showed what God had done for them. One board read, "I remember being homeless, addicted to drugs," and on the back it said, "Found God, and now I work for a home-less shelter." One said, "I remember being in prison, feel-ing hopeless and alone," and on the other side it said, "Found God and a wife, and now I work for a prison ministry." Each poster board had the same scenario: pain and heartache transformed to fullness and joy. All the while, "Amazing Grace" played in the background: "My chains are gone, I've been set free, my God, my Savior has ransomed me." See, God would just be another god if it weren't for stories like these, stories of redemption that could only come from a powerful Savior. It can only happen because He traded everything for a chance to win your heart. We each have an "I remember" time, a pain so deep it's worth writing down. But if you've found God, there's always a flip side. He's always whispering in your ear, "I made you to do great things for My Kingdom."

My card would read like this: "I remember addictions, heartache, and loneliness." But the back would say, "Redeemed, married, fulfilled, and happily serving high school kids just like me." Nothing says how great our God is more than scenarios such as these. We were all made for greater things, a chance to show the world the glory God deserves. Stories like these tell the world we've been through the dark but made it to the light. They tell the world that there is hope. Most of all, stories like these tell us we are not alone.

This Is Where the Whole Thing Went Wrong. . . .

Girls can be a little evil, especially high school girls. I hate to put it that way, but no other word describes how some girls can be. For those of you who are not evil, congrats. I was evil. Girls were scared of me, not because I was rough and tough, but because I was evil. If I didn't like someone, I would say it to her face. I didn't understand why honesty was so frowned upon. I had this theory that I was doing girls a favor by not lying to them. The way I saw it was you either openly hate someone or hate them and act like you love them. Occasionally I did play the other card, depending on what I could get from someone, but most of the time I was openly spiteful. There was one girl in our "group" who kissed my ex, and I blared the song "Homewrecker" in my car and pulled up next to her with another friend in the car singing it. Evil. I often made girls cry, and because I was "not emotional," I was never really invested in the drama.

As women we're given unique gifts that men don't have. These gifts often get misused; we use them for evil instead of good. Our vulnerability and need to be desired can push us to seek security in men, which can leave us heartbroken and needy. Our ability to read others can make us great liars and even better manipulators. Our ability to see wisdom in situations can also be used to hurt others with our knowledge. The strength God gave us to bear our burdens can quickly turn into bitterness and anger.

As I said before, I was always angry, and it was never my fault. I was able to manipulate situations so they best served me, and my rough exterior let me abuse myself while ignoring the consequences. Even though I didn't consider myself needy or vulnerable, I was always looking for someone to love and always getting my heart broken. My best friend and I expressed our anger by throwing sticks at trees when life was really hard. Weird, I know, but we needed an outlet for our emotions.

God gave us emotions for a reason, yet they can betray

us. My emotions lied when they told me I needed my first love physically; they told me I wouldn't be happy until we were together. I listened to those emotions for a long time. I believed my heart could never move on from him, but the heart is deceitful above all else (see Jeremiah 17:9). Because I had so mishandled my heart, I couldn't tell the difference between what was best for me and what would be a quick fix. Getting back together with him would have been a quick fix. I would have stopped hurting temporarily, but it would never have lasted. I would have had to go through the same pain over and over again until I forced my heart to move on.

Today I'm an emotional junkie; after finding God, I loved all these great feelings I discovered. I found a love with Ben that wasn't painful, and I would get high from our late-night talks and dreams about our future. I'm intoxicated by community, love, passion, and joy. I love movies that make me feel alive and songs that I can blare and sing along to. I love displays of love, and I think weddings are a good time to have a cry. I get high off the joy of life, which also means that the pain of life can throw me into a dark hole. I act out of whatever I feel. The feelings are real, though, and they mean something real, but they are meant to be filled by lasting things, not temporary fixes.

When I was sixteen, I hated feelings because they hurt. What I really hated was that my feelings revealed the truth about the lifestyle I protected so fiercely. My anger was a way to take control of the sadness I felt every day. If I took on a tough persona, I could ignore the fact that my heart was breaking a little bit every minute. If I could be stronger than my circumstances, then my life wasn't falling apart. If I could pretend I didn't need to be vulnerable, then I could stuff this deep desire to be known by someone, really known.

Recently I was substitute teaching in a middle school when I heard some girls talking about fighting another girl. I asked them if this was a common thing, and since I'm not their teacher, they spilled it all. They told story after story of girls getting in fistfights after school as a way to solve things. I tried to remind myself not to stare at them in disbelief. When did we get to the point where we have to solve arguments like guys? No offense to the boys, but one of the great things about being a woman is our ability to talk through things. My belief is that we have so denied our true nature, so forgotten the great things that make us unique, that we will do anything to be different. We will do anything to prove that we're strong enough to survive.

Since when has surviving meant physically fighting over a boy you won't even remember in five years? Most of these fourteen-year-old girls had been in fights, some of them forced by self-defense, but some were proud. They wanted the world to know they weren't scared of anything. Vulnerability gone bad; strength being abused, girls are fighting to deny who they really are. The idea is that if we can be as strong as men, then men won't hurt us. If we can prove we're worth the same, then they won't shatter our hearts and we won't spend another Friday night with a chick flick and a tub of Butterfinger ice cream.

String of Broken Hearts

ELIZABETH BENNET: BELIEVE ME. MEN ARE EITHER EATEN UP WITH ARROGANCE OR STUPIDITY. IF THEY ARE AMIABLE, THEY ARE SO EASILY LED THEY HAVE NO MINDS OF THEIR OWN WHATSOEVER.

MRS. GARDINER, *LAUGHING*: TAKE CARE, MY LOVE. THAT SAVORS STRONGLY OF BITTERNESS.
—*PRIDE AND PREJUDICE* (2005)

When you're bitter, it saturates every part of you. You can't isolate it to one part of your life; it leaks onto everything else. After my heart was broken, I set out to break everyone else's. I dated and cheated and carried a string of broken hearts as my prize. I was so bitter about the cards I had dealt myself that I sought revenge on the male race. I found boys to adore me, I made them feel they had me, and then I broke their hearts before they could break mine. It was twisted logic, but it was all I had. My first love wouldn't pay, so I made every other man pay.

Anytime I felt my heart start to slide into love, I called it quits or cheated so that they would have to break up with me. I was too broken to have anything left to give. I was too hurt to help anyone, so I took free handouts of love from any man who would offer, leaving little and gaining nothing.

There was a problem, though: breaking others doesn't heal your own life. Gossip doesn't make you feel better about your own faults. Sex doesn't make you feel more worthy of love, and denying who you are won't change how you were made. You can cover it, mask it, and try to outrun it, but God created you to be vulnerable. He created you to feel. He created you to love with a sense of abandonment. God created you with certain responsibilities as a woman, and you can't truly be who God made you to be unless you embrace how He has made you.

Men may have it slightly easier—and the emphasis here is on *may*. It doesn't matter. God has guaranteed us all a place; we don't have to fight for it. One day you will find a man who won't misuse your vulnerability or run away with your love. You'll find a man who knows he doesn't have to fight for his place in life. Together you can conquer the world with your ability to love fiercely and his ability to be strong, with his ferocious love for you and your strength to carry on.

God gave us our unique feminine traits to be matched with a man, not to overcome him. To become less of a woman would be to deny God's great calling for you. I'm not saying men can't be feminine or that women are the only ones who can be feelers. I have three brothers who are all "feelers," and it's one of the great things about them, yet they are also strong men in their relationships. Meanwhile, their wives have a unique perspective that my brothers often can't see. I have girlfriends who are not feelers and aren't as emotional, but they are wise and perceptive in their own ways. I don't know your personality, but I do know if you're denying who you are to prove something, you're fighting a losing battle. You will not gain anything by denying yourself the freedom to feel, to be vulnerable, or to love without boundaries.

My two-year-old nephew is a master manipulator; he will bat his beautiful blue eyes and tell you he loves you right before he asks for another piece of candy. He isn't allowed to have candy at home. I would say he doesn't know what he's doing, but he's smarter than that. He knows I can't refuse him. I can't say no to his precious two-year-old hug and sloppy kiss on my cheek. I always give in, because he knows what I want to hear, and I have what he wants.

Well, I wasn't much different at the age of sixteen than a manipulative two-year-old, and I wasn't an innocent child anymore. I knew who I needed to suck up to, which girls I had to pretend I liked, and how to get boys to give me what I wanted. High school is a food chain of sorts, except everyone is trying to get to the top, and people get eaten along the way. You have to meet a certain criteria to make it to the top, and somehow the people at the top get respect they often don't deserve.

One of my younger brother's friends was at a local Smoothie King, and he struck up a conversation with the girl at the counter. He learned she was my age and asked the girl if she knew me. Her response was classic: "Yeah, she's a b----." I couldn't have said it better myself. I was always climbing the food chain, and I didn't care who I hurt along the way as long as it wasn't me. Consequently, I had to make a lot of apologies when I changed, and I was constantly having to prove that I wasn't the same girl I used to be. At first, most people didn't understand; they thought the guy I was dating was making me change or that maybe I had joined a cult. But slowly I showed that I was a different person. My family was accepting, but my old friends didn't understand. I can't blame them, because I changed who I was quickly. But after a while they accepted the new me and moved past it.

Meanwhile, I had to relearn all the gifts that God gave me and how to use them for good instead of evil. Luckily, this time I was learning to trust God and wasn't navigating on my own. God was there to guide me and show me that I didn't have to be so harsh. I didn't have to build walls so high no one could get through. I didn't have to climb over people to get what I wanted. I just had to be patient and trust that in the end God knew better than I did. For me, finding God meant letting go of a lot of grudges and pain. I had to accept that I could never get retribution from those who had hurt me, but let me tell you firsthand that forgiveness is a great thing. I made amends with people I "hated" and found new friends along the way. I could never have done that alone. Fortunately, God never left my side.

There is a common theme throughout my story—if you haven't noticed: trading one thing in hopes for another. Sex for love, alcohol for community and happiness, smoking for relief, anorexia for control, beauty for attention, and on and on it goes. I didn't know where to take my desires, so I sought temporary satisfaction. I didn't realize there was another way to fill my desires, other things that would make me truly happy. The desires weren't the problem; it was how I was filling them that was. It is perfectly natural to want community, love, attention, security, and relief from pain, but I didn't realize there was another way to be satisfied, a way that was lasting and didn't cost me anything.

When I was living that life, the emotions felt so real. The joy I felt when I was drinking with my friends wasn't about the alcohol; it was about being involved in a group. My heart longs for community, but at sixteen I didn't know what to do with that, so I drank to be part of something. Then I fooled myself into believing that the bond we shared was real, that we all drank together because we were such great friends, that we had fun together because I was in the group, part of the crowd. The problem with the crowd is that you have to follow the crowd to be in it; your membership is conditional.

Most people don't want to be told that there's another way of life. No one wants to be reminded that they're unhappy. But if you prove you can be happy without drinking, then you're shattering the lie. My older brother did it, and he remained amazingly popular. But I chose a different route, one based on belonging and not on who I truly was. So after I was excommunicated from the group by my ex-boyfriend, most of my friends abandoned me. They weren't willing to give up the drinking to be by my side on Friday night, so I was left at home with the only people whose love wasn't conditional, my family.

If you aren't in a place of having to face your pain yet, you will be. At some point you'll hit a point where you're sobbing into your pillow as a song plays over you that you hoped would never make it to your sound track. Maybe you've already reached the point where you are ready to make changes in your life, and you're trying to communicate that to your old friends. They might tell you that you're a buzzkill or you're not fun anymore, but that's not even the tip of the iceberg. You're living proof that the lifestyle is fake, and no one wants that kind of reminder looming over them when they're trying to get a good buzz.

I am praying that you'll come to terms with the fact that you desperately need a Savior. It might not happen today. Then again, maybe it will.

CHAPTER 16

BRICK BY BRICK

WHEN BEN AND I were engaged, we went through pre-marital counseling to prepare for the adventure that is marriage. Since he was living in Texas and I was in Atlanta, we had four-hour sessions instead of a bunch of one-hour sessions. The first day the counselor sat us down and asked us each one prompt: "Tell me about your family." For four hours we went back and forth talking about what we wanted to do similarly to what our families did and what we wanted to do differently. I couldn't have imagined we could spend four hours talking about family, but when we were finished, we'd barely skimmed the surface.

Your family is where you learn everything. It's where

you learn who you are and what you're worth. It's where you pick up all your quirky habits and interesting traits. I would have liked to think Ben and I could start marriage fresh, but we couldn't. We were combining families, all my traits and all his traits meeting head-to-head under one roof. I didn't realize that family affected everything, even the things I didn't want it to. I didn't know that leaving butter out for days on end could be considered gross. I didn't know that messy floors would stress me out so much. I didn't know that the reality of being barefoot in the kitchen would make me want to vomit. Family teaches us everything. It will impact you in ways you don't even realize, until one day you wake up and discover you're just like your mother.

Family is a tricky thing. We're bound to people we don't always get along with, and so often we miss the joy that is family. We're a selfish society, caught up in what we can get. We don't like the fact that family requires loving without expecting to get something in return—at least I didn't. In my eyes, my family gave me nothing except a rule book to follow and brothers who annoyed me. I spent years abusing their love, but they waited for me with open arms. They loved me even though they got nothing in return. After I changed and we mended our relationships, I tried so hard to make up for lost time. I would come home from college for every birthday party, family event, and illness I could. When my mom was hurting, I rushed to her aid, and when my family was in trouble, I rallied the troops to fight through it. When my husband and I got married, I had a hard time leaving home because I was so invested in repairing the damage. My family had become my world, and I couldn't believe I'd missed out on these relationships for so long.

When I was in the midst of my rebellion, Satan had me convinced that my parents were the problem. I had to have a scapegoat because if I could see reality, if I could see that I was the problem, then I might stop self-destructing. I was the problem, though. My parents did nothing but parent, and for that I hated them. I wanted my freedom, which, I have to admit, at sixteen wasn't mine to grasp. I wanted my parents to let me make my mistakes and stay out of my life. I wanted them to let me drown. I was one of the lucky ones, though. My parents cared. Most of my friends' parents knew we drank, they knew we were having sex, they knew we did drugs, but they didn't seem to care.

The weird thing about being a teen is that you want someone to give you boundaries because you know deep down that you're hurting yourself. You know discipline will hurt, but if your parents care enough to discipline you, then they love you. If they love you enough to make the hard decisions, then they care about your well-being. If they punish you even when you kick and scream, then you mean something to them. Some parents like to think they're doing kids a favor by giving them "room to make mistakes," but that's selfishness with a fancy title. Some of my friends' parents wanted to be "cool," to let us drink at their houses, to smoke with us, but I'm sad to say many of their kids never came out of it. Whether the parents meant it or not, I have to believe most of my friends got the message that they weren't worth the headache that it takes to parent.

My parents weren't perfect, but they tried desperately to parent any way they could. They did everything to send the message that my life was worth more than this lifestyle and that I deserved more than I was allowing myself. My friends could see that. They often joked that they wanted my parents to adopt them. They loved being at my house, and I couldn't see why. I was so deceived that I couldn't see the greatest gift God had given me.

We often reject our families because we see something in them we don't want to have. Every kid has said, "When I get older, I'm never going to do what my parents have done." How many times have you heard a girl say, "I pray I don't end up like my mother"? It's because we can see the faults in our parents that remind us of our own faults. We're part of our parents, and for some of us that's very scary. You can avoid it and run from them, hoping you can achieve a different life, but you're a part of your family. You have half your mom and half your dad, and while that may be scary for you, it could also be great. While your differences may separate you, your similarities can bind you.

My mom and I used to have World War III in our house on a daily basis. She hated my attitude, and I hated how she knew everything. We would fight almost every day—unless we were shopping. Somehow, we always managed to get along then. It was only after I moved out that I realized we fought because we were so much alike. My mom and I have a similar story. It was only after I was away from her that I really learned to appreciate who she is and what she has done for me.

My relationship with my mom healed, but many never do. So many girls never learn the wonder that is their mother. Some women never realize that their mothers are more like them than anyone else. Isn't this why our mothers can drive us crazy? They are a glimpse of our futures and our faults. I have long wanted to repair the damage that's been done between mothers and daughters, to find a way to bridge the gap. I want to give advice that will heal all. I'm still waiting on God to show me how to do that, but right now all I have is what happened for my mom and me.

To my mother's credit, she always loved me. She didn't always like me, but she loved me. She went out of her way to love me even when I didn't deserve it. She loved me when she smelled cigarettes on my breath and found alcohol under my bed. She loved me when she found me drunk at two in the afternoon and when she saw me taking shots on spring break. (I should note here that I got punished for all those things, lovingly but very sternly.)

She loved me when I refused her love. She loved as Christ loved. Not only did she love me, but she made an effort to know me. She fed me breakfast in the morning and dinner at night. She left notes in my lunch when I had bad days and sat with me when I needed to talk. My mother realized something that many parents have forgotten: parents can be the number one influence in their children's lives. The distractions of life are just that—distractions—but deep down all kids want something more. They want a connection. Isn't that what technology is doing, giving us easier ways to connect with people like us? If a parent can form a connection, no matter how small, she'll make a lasting impact.

My mother modeled everything that I do now. I love my husband better because of her. And when I have kids, I'll mother as my mom mothered. My ways mimic my mother's because she was a lasting influence. Friendships will fall away, teachers will leave, pastors won't always get it right, but a parent has a platform that will never be replaced. It can be used wrongly or ignored, but either way what John Mayer sings is true:

> *Fathers, be good to your daughters*
> *Daughters will love like you do*
> *Girls become lovers who turn into mothers*
> *So mothers, be good to your daughters too.*
> —JOHN MAYER, "DAUGHTERS"

I'd like to add my own advice to all the daughters out there. First of all, forgive yourselves. The pain I caused my mother literally led her to end up in the hospital, but she would never tell you that part. She would tell you how I took care of her when she was sick. She would tell you how we laughed together. She only remembers the good. She is like God in that way. Asking your mom for forgiveness will get you a long way, but even more important is expressing your gratitude for the sacrifices she made daily. I don't know what kind of daughter you are or what kind of mother you have, but that doesn't change the fact that God has given you a chance at a unique relationship. My mother is who I call when life gets hard and when it is easy. She is my counselor and my best friend. She has wisdom no experts could impart, because no matter how much they know, they don't know me. My mother knows me. She saw me grow up, saw my failures and achievements, and can see more to come. It's crazy to me now how easily I traded that in; what I wouldn't give to get the wasted years back.

My dad was always the man I respected the most, and disappointing him was the greatest blow to my heart. I never respected the guys I dated, but my dad was a different story. It's been said that the best gift parents can give their kids is a good marriage, and I found that to be true. My dad spoiled my mom, but not in a bad kind of way. He wined and dined her like they were still two kids in love, and I often got grossed out by their touchy-feely behavior. Even when their marriage went through hard times and they were facing serious problems, I never questioned that I had two loving parents at home. When it came to their kids, they were a united front, rain or shine. Don't get me wrong—they argued, but we never questioned how much they loved each other. In a world that guarantees nothing, this was my saving grace.

Every Valentine's Day my dad brought home two sets of flowers, usually tulips for me and roses for my mom. I still have every card he gave me on Valentine's Day stored in a box under my bed. Even when I grew up and had boyfriends, I always looked forward to the flowers from my daddy. He was a constant, unlike any other man in my life during those years, and I reveled in his love. We'd go on long shopping trips, and over dinner we'd battle out life's great dilemmas. There was one thing I always loved about my dad: he valued my opinion. No matter where I was in life, he always wanted to know what I thought about things, because he cherished my opinion. He didn't blow me off as a silly girl or treat me like I was dumb. Instead, he taught me that I was a strong woman capable of carrying on a conversation with any man.

We had a tradition that every Christmas Eve he and I would go shopping for my mom's Christmas present. It was something I looked forward to each year. We'd spend the few weeks before "planning our attack" on the mall.

I don't know how many years we did this, but when I got married, my dad almost forgot my mom's Christmas present.

So many issues that girls have are blamed on their fathers. It's a lot of pressure for any man to take on, especially when high school girls can sound like they speak in their own language. We tend to blame all society's ills on broken families, but my dad loved me, cherished me, and respected me as a woman, and I still had issues. The greatest lesson I took away from my father was that I was smart and respectable and I had something to show the world. I was often dismissed for being silly and arrogant, but my dad believed in me. Over time, his belief in me gave me the courage to be who I wanted to be. I was never afraid to grab life by the horns, because my dad told me that I was one heck of a bull rider. A girl learns greatly from her father, not just in his words but in his silence. Silence from my dad meant he was disappointed in me, that I had shamed him, or that he wasn't proud of me, and that was worse than being grounded. My dad took an interest in my life, and for that, I valued him. I really never believed I would find a man like my father, and only after finding Ben did I realize I could never marry someone just like my father anyway, because we're so alike. My mom and I might have similar stories, but my dad and I have similar personalities.

CHAPTER 17

FROM HERE TO THERE

LOOKING BACK, IT all seems very clear how I ended up trapped in the rapids with no one who could save me but my King. I can see the slips, the tiny decisions that seemed insignificant, but in the moment I thought I was just living. I thought I was being a teenager, just discovering "who I was." The reality was that I was being lied to, daily, by myself. I was buying into the "me" mentality. My life was for me, was about me, and had one actress: me. I was center stage and lived with the notion that the world revolved around me. But I didn't have anyone to blame for my lifestyle but myself. I was the one downing the shots, making out with the boys, and doing the drugs.

No one held me down and forced me to do any of it, but for some reason I felt compelled to continue doing things that were harmful to me. The following passage helped me understand this slip into sin. God provided these verses to help us understand the process and learn what to avoid.

> They are darkened in their understanding and separated from the life of God because of the ignorance that is in them due to the hardening of their hearts. Having lost all sensitivity, they have given themselves over to sensuality so as to indulge in every kind of impurity, with a continual lust for more.
>
> EPHESIANS 4:18-19

"Darkened in Their Understanding . . ."

I feel like this is a nice way of saying you have lost your way. Suddenly, the things you thought you'd never do seem like no big deal. The laws of God seem insignificant and trivial. You feel as if you can't find your way in this world, so if you create your own rules, it will help you navigate. I love that it says *"darkened* in their understanding," because, make no mistake, believing the lies of your enemy, Satan, puts you in a very dark place. You feel clouded, as if someone has turned off the light in your head. Your feet start to feel unsteady, you feel misplaced in your own skin, and everything you thought you knew about your world suddenly feels wrong.

When my understanding was first darkened, I thought God was my problem. If I could just do all the things He told me not to do, then I'd be happy. I was a modern Eve, letting Satan speak the same lies to me that he said to Eve in the Garden. Satan told me, "God wants you to be lonely. He doesn't want you to have fun. Look at all the popular kids. They have so much fun, and you don't have a lot of friends. Don't you want to fall in love? Doesn't God want you to be happy?" With each lie I became more indignant, breathing them in like they were truth. I put on my stubborn face and started to echo Satan's lies with, "Yeah! Good point!" I was so deceived, my understanding was darkened.

"Separated from the Life of God . . ."

Once your understanding has been darkened, it's easy to separate yourself from the life of God. God is the God of light and truth, and when you believe the lies of the enemy, then you can easily slip away from God's plan. When I started to buy the lies, I stopped going to Bible study, stopped talking to my Christian friends, found church irrelevant, and blamed all my problems on church and God. He seemed to have nothing for me, but only because I slipped away from His plan and His heart. I thought people just didn't understand. I wanted freedom, and I wanted to be left alone. My brother Taylor's sweet girl-friend always tried to reach out to me. She would send me the most thoughtful notes about how she was praying for me and would love to be friends. I would laugh and tell my friends, "I don't know what she's praying for. I'm doing just fine." I was blind to the truth and separated from the life of God.

I've often struggled with the question of whether I was really saved before my great rebellion. Did I ever really accept Christ? Did I truly understand all that Jesus had to offer before I ran so far away? I don't know, but I do know that I never really knew Him like I should have. What I understand about God now means I can never go back to the darkness. Struggle and question I might, but I don't think I could ever return to a life totally separated from God. God is so captivating, so amazing, so fulfilling that my old life seems like a distant memory.

"The Hardening of Their Hearts . . ."

If you don't know whether you're being deceived, here's a quick way to find out: check your heart. Does it break when you hear of world tragedies? Do you ache when you see a homeless man on the side of the interstate? Do you well up with tears when you see an older man eating alone? (Okay, maybe that's just me.) Does world hunger bother you? Do you want to help those in need? Do you want to listen to your friends when they hurt? Do you want to serve the help-less? Do you want to share the gospel with those who don't know the truth? Do you care enough about God's children to give up your own comfort and wealth?

Or are you constantly thinking about you? Do you wonder when the conversation will turn to your dreams and life? Do you pray that God never calls you to a for-eign mission field? Do you reason away the problems of the helpless with the excuse that they have to live with the consequences of their decisions? Do you care more about your own agenda than God's? Do you hope He takes care of you before He gets to all the orphans? Do you change the channel when the hurting children in other countries come on TV? Do you wonder where God is in the world's hurt but refuse to serve the hurting?

I can only ask these questions because I've gone through the same thing, where I wanted to lift high my agenda and to forget the rest of the world. For a time, I lived in a world that I felt revolved around me and my hurts, and anything outside of that was irrelevant. I was cold, bitter, and hard hearted. It's easy to fall into. The tiny worlds we create for ourselves are constantly generating the message that we, as individuals, matter more than everyone else. But what if we all lived in that lie? What if we all took on our own agendas and forgot the needs of the world? What if the orphans never got adopted and the brokenhearted never had a shoulder to cry on? Scary, right? Satan would love that! He would love nothing more than to convince everyone that we need not worry about anyone besides ourselves. If you can't see past your own fingertips, then your heart is hardened, and a hard heart is deadly.

There were plenty of times during my high school years that I thought my life was over. I thought I couldn't live another day with the hurt (that I caused myself), and I have one-too-many drafted suicide letters to prove it. I couldn't see past my tiny world. When you've built your life around your wants and needs and then things start crumbling, you get caught under the rubble. I felt trapped, unaware that I was simply caught underground and avoiding the ladder to light. There was a whole world outside my tiny hole, but I just couldn't see it.

"Every Kind of Impurity . . ."

When your understanding is darkened, you're separated from the life of God. Your heart is hardened, and you search for love in all the wrong places. You lose the sensitivity or discernment to know the difference between love and lust, so you try a little bit of everything. Relationships that leave you wanting, one-night stands that leave you lonely, kisses that mean nothing, and anything else that imitates love. You give yourself over to lust and hope it might turn into love. It might not even be your lust. Maybe it's someone else's, but you keep hoping that it might turn into something fulfilling and lasting, like one of those great romantic comedies where they fall into bed and then fall into love. Not how it works in the real world!

If you're giving yourself over without the foundation of commitment, then you'll end up more hardened than you were before you met Mr. Good-Enough-for-Right-Now. Don't be fooled by your hardened heart. You don't need another man; you need a Savior to remind you why you were sensitive to the things of God to begin with. Don't let your senses become numbed by your surroundings or by what others tell you. The morals you held tightly to yesterday are still the same today, no matter what Satan is trying to convince you of.

I was convinced I wouldn't have sex. It was out of the question. I might have fooled around, maybe fallen in love, but sex was for the confines of marriage. I told myself that at fifteen, before I really immersed myself in my popular lifestyle. After a year of drinking, a few of my friends were having sex. Then I met a boy and lost a significant amount of my sensitivity, and suddenly it was "just" a Friday night make out, "just" a hookup, "just" sex. Before I knew it, I had given over to every whim, every bad idea, every chance at love, and for what cause? I was broken and desperately lonely, and I had a reputation that was as dirty as my heart.

"A Continual Lust for More"

Let that sink in. *A continual lust for more.* It will never be enough; whatever you're addicted to, it will never be enough. Hear me loud and clear: *it will never be enough.* If there ever could be enough, there wouldn't be rehab, people wouldn't die of overdoses, and broken hearts wouldn't come in every shape and size. Whatever you're chasing, it will never be enough.

When I first started drinking, I only needed three shots to be drunk. I was skinny and young, so I prided myself on how little I had to drink in order to get a good buzz. I'd take the shots all in a row, preferring the drunkenness to come on fast and strong, and then I'd be happy for a few hours. After six months of drinking, I needed five shots to have the same effect. After a year, I needed a little more than six. It kept going on that way so that by senior year I was drinking ten to twelve shots of straight vodka a night. It was never enough. I started smoking because I couldn't get drunk at school and I needed something to make me feel different. It still wasn't enough, and Satan knew it never would be. His plan was that I would drink myself to death. I could have, and a few times I almost did, but for some reason God decided I could do the world some good through my mess of a life.

When I started having sex, I told myself it would just be that one guy, just my first love, and I wouldn't have sex again until I was married. But then we broke up, and the other stuff wasn't enough. I ended up sleeping with my next boyfriend because it was never enough.

Whatever you can't let go of, trust me when I tell you it will never be enough. The drugs will fade and you'll need more, the buzz will wear off and you'll need another drink, the moment will end and you'll be more alone than before, the numbness will subside and you'll feel pain again. It will never be enough. That's why Jesus says that He is the living water (see John 7:37-38). He is the only thing that will ever be enough. Drink Him in, let His Word fill you, and let His love satisfy the need your soul has. Let His graciousness heal your hardened heart, and let His grace cover your wounds.

Don't believe the lies. Please listen to your Savior's sweet voice and trust Him.

Whenever people hear that I am writing a book, they ask, "What's it about?" I tell them I want to help teenage girls see truth. The follow-up question is always the same: "Is it a self-help book?" I pray that it is not. I'm not a trained counselor, and I don't claim to know anything divine. I just know a story that begins in darkness and ends in brilliant light. I know a story that beats all the odds and proves that God is a God who is mighty to save. One of my favorite things about Jesus is that He was a storyteller; He took life lessons and told them in a way that people could grasp. He told them in story form. I might not remember everything in the book of Romans, but I know all the Bible stories I was taught as a child.

Stories resonate in ways that simple advice cannot. I believe it's because we all want to know someone understands; we want to know that other people are going down the same path we are, because sometimes the path is dark, and when it's dark and you think you're alone, life is scary. I wrote this to tell you that you're not alone. I wrote this because you need to know that God can use you despite your past, despite whatever lies you might have embraced, and more than that, He desperately wants to use you. He can make you squeaky clean, and while it might take a Brillo pad to do so, let me promise you it is worth it in the end.

The Prodigal Son is a story most of us have heard, but no matter how many times I hear it, I always get choked up in the end when the father runs out to meet his son, despite his child's wretched failures (see Luke 15:11-32). If you don't understand why God could ever love you like that, then you've missed something huge. He is your Father, and while some earthly parents have really screwed up, God has a divine devotion to you that withstands every circumstance. He knows where you've been. He knows you have squandered His gifts to you. And yet He comes running. He knows where your head has been laid, and He knows you have broken His rules. And yet He comes running. He knows you have abandoned His love at times and spit on

His blessings. And still He comes running. He will always come running. He doesn't sit at the end of the driveway, arms crossed, tapping one foot, waiting to give a lecture. He runs at you full force until you collide with His amazing love. He weeps with you for your hurt, He comforts you with gifts you haven't earned, and He takes you into His arms. You belong safely nuzzled in your Father's arms, not in the arms of a stranger or in the chains of sin. He will clean your wounds and cover your shame. He will bless your return home to Him, even if yesterday you were lying with the pigs. That's what your heavenly Father does.

Writing this book taught me something I thought I already knew but I hadn't really grasped: God is not human. I know that sounds elementary, but I tend to view God through my human eyes. I think, *How could He love me when I have been so sinful?* And the answer is, because He's not human. How could He forgive me when I have done nothing to earn it? Because He is God. How could He love me that much? Because *He is God*. He doesn't wait until we've earned it, because He doesn't expect us to earn it. He doesn't give lectures, because He isn't on a power trip. Everything He does is for us. He is already God. He made everything we see, and He commands it. He doesn't need us for an ego trip. He just wants to love us. I know it doesn't make any sense, but it doesn't have to.

When was the last time you asked your dog to talk? I'm not crazy, I promise, but think about it. You don't ask your dog to do something it clearly cannot do. The creature is incapable of speaking, so you don't yell at it when it doesn't speak. Just as you would show grace to your dog, so God shows grace to us. We're not perfect, and God knows this. He knows we'll sin, and He knows we'll fail, because ever since sin entered the world, humans have been incapable of perfection. God doesn't expect you to be blameless on your own; He expects you to run after Him full force, because that's what will give you life. He came because we need a Savior. It is a fact of life. So don't hold God to human standards. Just follow Him, love Him, let Him teach you, and let Him be your one and only God. That is as close to perfection as you or any of us will ever get.

Trade in your human desires for Someone, Something greater. And, trust me, not only will God fulfill your desires, He'll give you so much more. Try Him—and live!

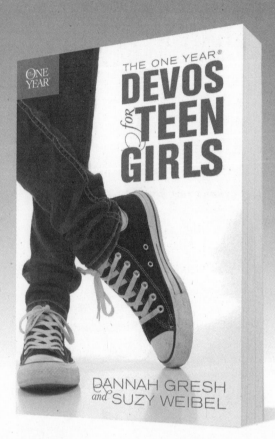

Online Discussion *guide*

TAKE *your* TYNDALE READING EXPERIENCE *to the* NEXT LEVEL

A FREE discussion guide for this book is available at bookclubhub.net, perfect for sparking conversations in your book group or for digging deeper into the text on your own.

www.bookclubhub.net

You'll also find free discussion guides for other Tyndale books, e-newsletters, e-mail devotionals, virtual book tours, and more!